SMA

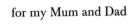
for my Mum and Dad

Neil D'Souza

SMALL MIRACLE

OBERON BOOKS
LONDON

First published in 2007 by Oberon Books Ltd
521 Caledonian Road, London N7 9RH
Tel: 020 7607 3637 / Fax: 020 7607 3629
e-mail: info@oberonbooks.com
www.oberonbooks.com

A catalogue record for this book is available from the British
Library.

Cover design by Oberon Books.

ISBN: 1 84002 784 3 / 978-1-84002-784-6

Printed in Great Britain by Antony Rowe Ltd, Chippenham.

Characters

ARJUN, 34

MEERA, 60s

BRONAGH, 39

SADIE, 13

BARRY, late 50s / early 60s

Note:
Hanh means 'Yes' in Hindi;
Chuppals mean 'Sandals'

Small Miracle was first performed by the Mercury Theatre Company at the Mercury Theatre, Colchester, on 1 June 2007, with the following cast:

ARJUN Kulvinder Ghir

MEERA Souad Faress

BRONAGH Gina Isaac

SADIE Ella Vale

BARRY Peter Dineen

Director Janice Dunn

Designer Chloe Lamford

Act One

SCENE 1

Set: a caravan park.

A caravan is parked stage left, in a neat concrete bay, angled so that we see the side of it – a curtained window then a door upstage with steps under it. The vehicle painted white except for a brown stripe that runs along the side of it, broken only by the legend JOURNEY'S END. On the same side, further downstage, there is a round plastic table with three plastic chairs. The table is set up for a small gathering – breadsticks, dips. The upstage right corner is where the women's toilet/shower facilities are: the face of a unit and a door marked WC. Downstage on the same side is a four-pointed sign, indicating the direction of things offstage: 'Shrine' (stage centre), 'Office' (downstage right), 'Toilets' (upstage right) and 'Pitch and Putt' (upstage left). Outside the concrete bay, the floor is a neat patch of grass, perfectly square, and the background may suggest other such enclosures, evenly spaced, mostly empty, beyond which lie fields and then an infinite, almost unreal expanse of cloudy blue heavens. SADIE – thirteen – is sitting at the table trying out different ring tones on her mobile phone. Sometimes there is dark confidence about this girl, whilst at other times she's just a playful child. A light shines on her from the direction of the shrine – the sun coming out from behind clouds? After some time, BARRY emerges from the WC. He lights a roll-up cigarette.

BARRY: Are you after having a shower there?

SADIE: What?

BARRY: Are you after having a shower?

SADIE: No.

BARRY: Cos there's water all over the floor in there.

SADIE: It wasn't me.

BARRY: Cos when you've a shower, you've to put the curtain inside of the base.

SADIE: I know.

BARRY: Otherwise the water goes all over like.

SADIE: I know.

BARRY: It goes all over the floor.

7

SADIE: I know.

BARRY: Cos you could slip and crack your head there now.

SADIE: What?

BARRY: You could slip and crack your head and wind up in hospital.

SADIE: I know.

BARRY: You could wind up in hospital with brain damage.

SADIE: What?

BARRY: Another job for me now, as if I haven't got enough jobs.

SADIE: Like what?

BARRY: What?

SADIE: Like what have you got to do?

BARRY: Many things.

SADIE: Like sitting in there watching telly?

BARRY: What?

SADIE: Like sitting in there watching Baywatch?

BARRY: I was manning the phone.

SADIE: Do you like Baywatch?

BARRY: Sure, I don't know what was on. I was manning the phone.

SADIE: Sure, the phone never rings.

BARRY: It still has to be manned.

SADIE: Why?

BARRY: Cos it may ring.

SADIE does a long, agonised silent scream.

Something the matter?

SADIE: Bored.

BARRY: Lucky you.

SADIE: Nothing happens here.

BARRY: It does.

SADIE: What?

BARRY: Just last week there, a whole crowd of Germans arrived up, fourteen of them, fourteen Germans all wanting to know about the shrine, and where to buy toothpaste –

SADIE: Did you contain your excitement?

BARRY: And today it's the toilet. Blocked. Sure, it was yer one who was complaining. The Indian lady in your party. The Indian lady in the Indian dress.

SADIE: That's Meera. She's my granny from London.

BARRY: She's your granny?

SADIE: Yeah.

BARRY: She's your granny?

SADIE: Yeah.

BARRY: She's your grandmother?

SADIE: Yeah.

Beat.

BARRY: She's your grandmother?

SADIE: Got a problem with that?

BARRY: No...I'm just wondering.

SADIE: Why? Cos she's black?

BARRY: No.

SADIE: Why then?

BARRY: Just. (*Beat.*) Sure, we get all types here these days – black, white, purple. Sure, I know a Muslim...in Charlestown.

Beat.

SADIE: Bum us a fag, will ya?

BARRY: What? How old are you?

SADIE: Sixteen.

BARRY: You are not.

SADIE: I am!

BARRY: Will I ask your mother?

SADIE: Ok fifteen and a half...ok fourteen...ok...thirteen.

BARRY: Is that your final offer?

SADIE: Yeah.

BARRY: You're very bold.

SADIE: As Mam says you don't get anywhere in this world hiding in a corner.

BARRY: Does she know you smoke?

SADIE: Yes.

BARRY: Will I ask her so?

SADIE: No.

BARRY: I've a good mind to.

SADIE: Do that and I'll tell everyone you were watching Baywatch.

BARRY: I was manning the phone.

SADIE: I'll tell them what you were thinking.

BARRY: I was manning the phone.

SADIE: Cos I know what you were thinking. I know what's in your mind.

BARRY: What?

SADIE: (*With meaning.*) I know things.

BARRY: What things?

SADIE: I know you're Sad. I know you're all alone.

Beat.

BARRY: Are you a lula?

SADIE: What?

BARRY: Bit funny in the head?

SADIE: Don't laugh at me!

BARRY: Jesus we've a right loony here.

SADIE: (*Aggressive.*) I said don't laugh!

ARJUN arrives back from the shops carrying a plastic bag and talking on his mobile.

ARJUN: (*Into mobile.*) Yeah. Yeah. Yeah. Yeah. (*To SADIE.*) What's going on?

SADIE: Nothing!

ARJUN: (*Still into mobile.*) Yeah. Yeah. Yeah. (*To BARRY.*) Is she… Is she…?

BARRY: (*Putting out cigarette, going into the toilet.*) No, I was just sorting out the loo –

ARJUN: (*Into mobile.*) Sorry. Yeah. Yeah. Oh no, no, no. (*To SADIE.*) You're supposed to be making an effort?

SADIE: I'm here, amn't I?

ARJUN: (*Into mobile.*) Right Yeah. Yeah. I'm on the mobile anyway so… Cheers Phil. Cheers Phil. Yeah. Yeah. (*Pause.*) Yeah. (*ARJUN hangs up. He looks stressed. Beat.*)

SADIE: Are we on holiday?

ARJUN: Yeah.

SADIE: Is that what this is?

ARJUN: Yeah.

SADIE: Cos Angelina Curry's gone to EuroDisney.

ARJUN: We can go to EuroDisney next year.

SADIE: Next year we could all be dead.

ARJUN: Don't say that.

SADIE: (*Growing excitement.*) I'm so bored I am considering killing myself. How would I do it though? Eat a bottle? Then all the bits would slash me internal organs, and blood would come pouring out my mouth, or stick my tongue in an electric socket. Can you imagine it? (*She sticks out her tongue, goes into violent convulsions.*) No, I know: stick two pencils up my nose right, one in each hole and then head butt the table. I'd have to do it a few times though, to get the pencils deep enough to pierce the brain.

ARJUN: That's not funny.

She grabs two breadsticks and puts one in each nostril.

SADIE: I'll do it, Arjun. I'll do it.

ARJUN: Sadie!

SADIE: I don't want to, but I will.

ARJUN: Stop that.

SADIE: Give me one good reason?

ARJUN: It's unhygienic.

SADIE: I'm about to kill myself here!

ARJUN: People have to eat those Sadie.

SADIE: (*On her knees to him.*) Do something! Do something! For God's sake man!

ARJUN: And do not put them back in the glass.

She takes the breadsticks out of her nose.

SADIE: Thanks a million, Arjun.

ARJUN: You shouldn't joke about those things.

SADIE: Who's joking? (*SADIE makes to go.*)

ARJUN: Where are you going?

SADIE: To see my friend.

ARJUN: Which friend?

SADIE: A girl I was talking to in the field.

ARJUN: You can't.

SADIE: Why not?

ARJUN: You know why: we're having a party for the priest.

SADIE: I'm bored, Arjun.

ARJUN: Read your magazine.

SADIE: It's boring.

ARJUN: Just stay put.

SADIE: Is that an order?

ARJUN: Yes.

SADIE: You can't give me orders. You're not my Da.

ARJUN: Sadie!

SADIE: You going to hit me as well?

ARJUN: No, of course not.

SADIE: He used to hit me.

ARJUN: I know.

SADIE: It damaged me emotionally.

ARJUN: Just, sit tight.

SADIE: And be bored?

ARJUN: Yes.

> *SADIE sits down and looks bored and miserable. ARJUN takes two bottles of wine out of the bag and puts them on the table.*

> I didn't want to come here either Sadie, but it's just one day.

> *SADIE sulks.*

> We all have to do things we don't want to do, Sadie. That's life. I am an insurance developer in the financial services sector. I get up at five-thirty every morning – do I want to do that? And this thing tonight, this vigil that Mum wants me to go to, apparently it goes on all night? Do I want to do that?

> *SADIE continues to sulk.*

> Are you sulking? Don't sulk. Ok. Sulk. (*He pulls out a notebook.*) I had a vivid dream last night involving druids bathing me. I must write it down.

> *He sits down and begins to write. SADIE continues to sulk. BRONAGH comes out of the caravan with stuff, which she lays out on the table. She clocks SADIE.*

BRONAGH: What's up with her?

ARJUN: She's bored.

BRONAGH: Lighten up darling. We're having a party.

> *SADIE looks even more bored, miserable and annoyed.*

> No? Then rinse these glasses for me.

> *SADIE looks bored, miserable, annoyed and indignant.*

> I thought you were bored. I'm giving you something to do.

SADIE: (*Sudden outburst.*) Why do I have to do everything round here?

BRONAGH: It speaks!

SADIE: Didn't I wash up after breakfast?

BRONAGH: What do you want a medal?

SADIE: I don't even want to be here.

BRONAGH: Well, you are here. So, make the best of it.

SADIE: This place is a fucking dump!

BRONAGH: And do not use language like that.

SADIE: That's what you said on the phone to Nora last week.

BRONAGH: Listening to my conversation, were you?

SADIE: That's what you said.

BRONAGH: What I said is neither here nor there.

SADIE: What does that mean?

BRONAGH: It means go and wash the glasses.

SADIE: I can't. Not while I've got this stuff on my hand.

BRONAGH: Wash it off then.

SADIE: It doesn't wash off, Meera said. It's a tattoo.

BRONAGH: It better not be.

SADIE: It stays on for weeks.

BRONAGH: Just go and wash the glasses, will you?

SADIE: No.

SADIE walks off.

BRONAGH: Sadie! SADIE!

SADIE has gone. BRONAGH is about to go after her.

ARJUN: Leave her. Let her go.

BRONAGH: (*As she lays more stuff on the table.*) Is it was my fault?
(*Referring to SADIE.*) What am I supposed to do? Hit her? Like
Stuart did? You hit a child, you take it's spirit away. I know
that well enough. Though sometimes I'm tempted. Like when
we when we were making this stuff. Anything your Mother
said, she would do, but if I asked her to do one thing it was
'Why? Why? Why?' Honestly I could have brained her with
a brick. And your mother filling her head with stories of the

14

Virgin Mary, the Hindu Gods. I made these. (*She opens a container and sniffs it.*) I hope they're ok. They should be. Your Mother watched me the whole time. Told me exactly what to do and when.

ARJUN: She doesn't mean it.

BRONAGH: It's fine, Arjun. (*Laughing.*) Wait till you see what she gave me this morning? (*BRONAGH riffles in a bag under the table. She pulls out a plastic ornament – a picture of the Knock Apparition, Mary, the Saints, witnesses, angels. The whole thing encased in fairy lights, and an inscription underneath.*)

ARJUN: (*Taking it, reading.*) 'Bless Our Home.'

BRONAGH: For the new house she said. (*BRONAGH switches it on: the Virgin begins to glow, the fairy lights begin to flash and Ave Maria – the song of Lourdes version – plays music box style.*) She said to put it above the front door.

ARJUN: (*Laughing.*) What did you say?

BRONAGH: (*Laughing.*) Thank you. (*BRONAGH turns it off the ornament.*) I don't get it, Arjun. Why did she drag us here?

ARJUN: It's the Virgin, isn't it? She loves the Virgin Mary.

BRONAGH: But, she's a Hindu. Are Hindus allowed to love the Virgin Mary?

ARJUN: Don't ask me.

BRONAGH: But, here of all places. I can't keep a straight face.

ARJUN: Don't think I didn't see you smirking in church.

BRONAGH: It was gospel according to St Luke. You know where you do the sign of the cross on your forehead, mouth and heart. We always used to pretend it was picking the scalp, picking the nose and eating the bogey.

ARJUN: Next time I'll put you over my knee.

BRONAGH: I'll knee you in the bollocks.

ARJUN: Yeah?

BRONAGH: Yeah.

ARJUN: Come here and say that. Come here!

She comes over to him. He holds her.

15

Two weeks in a caravan and not a hotel room in sight.

BRONAGH: It was your idea.

ARJUN: I thought it would bring all us closer together.

BRONAGH: It's done that.

ARJUN: Maybe we can get a hotel room in Galway.

BRONAGH: Just the one?

ARJUN: No, one for Mum and Sadie. One for you and me.

BRONAGH: What for?

He kisses her. They kiss.

MEERA: (*From inside the caravan.*) Bronwyn! Can you give me a hand one minute?!

ARJUN: What did she call you?

BRONAGH: Bronwyn.

ARJUN: Didn't you correct her?

BRONAGH: About eight million times.

MEERA: It's burning Bronwyn!

BRONAGH goes into the caravan. MEERA pops her head out of the door.

Back son? You got the wine?

ARJUN: Two bottles.

MEERA: Good. Help me down will you?

ARJUN helps her down. It's a painful process owing to MEERA's leg for which she uses a crutch. As ARJUN helps her down, she exclaims in Hindi under her breath in pain: 'O Ma! Meri Ma! Hey Bhagwan!' [O Mother! My Mother! Hey God!]

Everything ready? Good. Soon he'll be here. Where's Sadie?

ARJUN: Playing with her friend.

MEERA: Now she is playing? Why is she playing now?

ARJUN: She's only in the field, Mum.

MEERA: My back is hurting and all night I had no sleep. It's that bed. It's not good for my back. I like to sleep on hard beds, but this bed is soft. Why did you give me such a soft bed?

ARJUN: I tried all the beds in all the caravans they had.

MEERA: These caravan beds. Cheap beds they are. Rubbish beds they are.

ARJUN: Why don't you sit down?

MEERA: No.

ARJUN: Rest.

MEERA: Rest In Peace. (*Beat.*) Last night, I dreamt of your Father. Standing in the garden he was, in the dead of night, his face blank like a mask, and beckoning me (*She demonstrates ghostly beckoning.*) beckoning me like this into the garden, into the darkness…

ARJUN: Perhaps he wants you to mow the lawn.

MEERA: Hut! When I'm gone, will you be laughing then?

ARJUN: Where are you going?

MEERA: Far away.

ARJUN: Cork?

MEERA: Further.

ARJUN: Wexford?

MEERA: Who knows? Who cares? As long as I can see you settled and happy – you and Bronwyn.

ARJUN: Bronagh.

MEERA: What?

ARJUN: Bronagh, not Bronwyn.

MEERA: Who is Bronagh?

ARJUN: Her name is Bronagh, not Bronwyn.

MEERA: Is it? Why didn't she say? Well, as long as the two of you are settled and happy – you and Brondagh. Then, I can go on my way. On my long, long journey into the dark, dark night.

Beat.

ARJUN: That's a cheery thought.

MEERA: What?

ARJUN: Nothing. (*Beat.*) You know this thing tonight. This vigil.

MEERA: What about it?

ARJUN: You know you have to stay up all night.

MEERA: That why it's called an All Night Vigil, Arjun.

ARJUN: But, what's it in aid of?

MEERA: It for the Virgin, isn't it? So nice it is, Father was telling me. You all sit there in the Apparition Chapel in the dead of night and pin drop silence there is. Not a sound to be heard.

ARJUN: What do you do though?

MEERA: You think, you pray, or just watch the statues. You know how many people saw her that day in 1876, Arjun? Fifteen. Can you imagine it? Fifteen people standing, watching her for three hours in pouring rain? (*Beat.*) You saw the picture I bought for the house?

ARJUN: Yes.

MEERA: You should put it above the front door.

ARJUN: We'll see.

MEERA: That's the best place for it.

ARJUN: We'll see.

MEERA: Above the front door is the best place.

ARJUN: We haven't even completed on the house yet.

MEERA: What other place is there?

ARJUN: I don't know.

MEERA: Where would you put it?

ARJUN: I'm not sure.

MEERA: Tell me where you would put it?

ARJUN: I don't know.

MEERA: No, give me your idea.

ARJUN: (*Sharp.*) I don't know.

MEERA: Why are you tense?

> *BRONAGH comes out of the caravan wearing oven gloves, carrying hot rice from the oven.*

BRONAGH: Mind out it's hot.

ARJUN clears a space on the table. BRONAGH puts the tray down.

MEERA: You've taken the rice out?

BRONAGH: Yes.

MEERA: And the chicken's not burning?

BRONAGH: No.

MEERA: I don't want it to burn.

BRONAGH: No.

MEERA: Nothing worse than burnt food.

BRONAGH: I know.

MEERA: Even dogs won't eat it then.

BRONAGH: It's not burning Meera, I promise.

ARJUN: What time's this priest getting here?

MEERA: Three o'clock he said. Such nice man. Father Hill – a real human being. So interested in India, in Indian food, I said, 'Come! Eat! I can't promise a big feast because I'm not in my own kitchen in London, but what I can, I'll do.'

The WC half-flushes several times. BARRY emerges from the toilet with a plunger. He stands there seething.

ARJUN: Still blocked?

BARRY: It's like a bring and buy sale down there: sweet wrappers, cigarettes. That's why I put the sign up, but does anybody read the sign? Well, here I am again elbow deep in other people's shit and it's not nice.

ARJUN: Why don't you have a drink?

BARRY: No, I won't intrude.

ARJUN: You're not intruding, is he?

MEERA smiles uncertainly.

BARRY: To be honest I could do with one the day I've had. I'll just wash up.

BARRY goes off taking mop, bucket and plunger.

MEERA: Arre?! What are you doing?

ARJUN: What?

19

MEERA: It's for the priest, Arjun.

ARJUN: He's only having a glass of wine.

MEERA: He'll stay for ten bottles.

ARJUN: No, he won't.

MEERA: This morning, seven o'clock I went in there to ask him something, drinking he'd been.

ARJUN: How do you know?

MEERA: I could smell it on his breath.

ARJUN: He's alright, Mum.

MEERA: He's the janitor.

ARJUN: He's the manager of the caravan park.

MEERA: Hut! Some manager! I can't believe it. I go to all this trouble and you invite the janitor. Fine! Invite them all – tramps and hobos!

ARJUN: Shall I open the wine?

MEERA: (*Snaps.*) Do what you want!

BRONAGH: You'll love Galway Meera. It's a good spot, you know, lots of music in the pubs.

MEERA: I don't go to pubs.

BRONAGH: Well, there's lots to see anyway – the cathedral.

MEERA: At my age, what is there to see?

BRONAGH: Or else the drive out to Connemarra is breathtaking.

MEERA: Too much sitting in the car makes me feel like vomiting.

ARJUN: Shall I open the wine?

MEERA: Why are you asking me?

ARJUN: Because I don't want to do the wrong thing again.

MEERA: I went to all this trouble, all this trouble –

ARJUN: Look, I didn't know –

MEERA: (*Sudden, explosive.*) YOU NEVER FUCKING KNOW.

Beat.

BRONAGH: Will I put this back in the oven?

MEERA: Just leave it.

BRONAGH: I'll put it back.

MEERA: (*Snap.*) Leave it! (*Beat.*) Such nice holidays we used to have, no Arjun? Me, you, your Daddy. Remember we went to Spain that time? That was a real holiday. A real fun time. Remember you asked for Melecoton in the restaurant? You'd seen it on the menu. Melecoton! Melecoton! You thought it was some fancy dessert! And in the end they brought you a peach. Oh the times we had. The laugh. Gone. All gone.

BARRY rushes on.

BARRY: I think you should come.

ARJUN: What's up?

BARRY: It's the girl. She's in the field. She's not well.

Blackout.

SCENE 2

Dusk. The same day. The light is fading, and the caravan park lights are on. The party stuff has been cleared away. ARJUN is sitting on the caravan step writing in a notebook. MEERA and SADIE are sitting at the table. MEERA is finishing off the mehendi (henna tattoo) on SADIE's hand. There is a portable stereo on the grass playing some Hindi music. MEERA hums along to it as she paints. BRONAGH calls to ARJUN from inside the caravan. Leaving his book on the step, he goes inside. SADIE sways to the music.

SADIE: I like this one.

MEERA: Hold still, darling.

SADIE: Ok, darling.

MEERA: Making fun of me?

SADIE: No, darling.

> *MEERA flicks some water on SADIE's nose. SADIE wants to retaliate.*

MEERA: Ah! Ah! You want to ruin this?

SADIE: That's not fair.

MEERA: Life's not fair, darling.

21

SADIE: (*Referring to music.*) So, what's this one about?

MEERA: Love. Same like the rest. It's from a film – 'Waqt'. You know what 'Waqt' means? Time. It's about a man who has a wife, three young sons and a business and everything is going fine. Then one day there is an earthquake and he loses everything – wife, sons, all.

SADIE: Dead?

MEERA: No, lost. He wanders the streets for many years in search of them.

SADIE: Is there not like a Victim Support Centre?

MEERA: No.

SADIE: That's a sad story.

MEERA: Aren't they the best ones? Growing up in Bombay, we used to go for all the movies – my sister and I. We'd sit there crying in the dark. But, most of all at the happy moments we used to cry. This film has a happy ending.

SADIE: He finds them?

MEERA: After many years.

SADIE: So, it all works out in the end?

MEERA: Hanh! In the movies. (*MEERA has finished.*) There! Now, let it dry.

SADIE: And you reckon it will stay on for a couple of weeks?

MEERA: Depends how often you wash it.

SADIE: I want it to last forever.

MEERA: Ho! As it is your mother wasn't too pleased with me!

SADIE: She can get stuffed.

MEERA: Don't say that.

SADIE: Why not?

MEERA: She's your mother.

SADIE: I can't wait till I'm old enough to live in a house with all my friends.

MEERA: Friends are nothing. When your luck is down, friends disappear. Only family are there for you. Never forget that.

Beat.

SADIE: Are you Hindu, Meera?

MEERA: Hanh.

SADIE: I wish I was Hindu.

MEERA: Why?

SADIE: Cos I like the clothes.

MEERA: You can still wear the clothes.

SADIE: Can I? (*Indicating forehead.*) Can I have one of those things?

MEERA: A bindi?

SADIE: What's it mean?

MEERA: It's my third eye.

SADIE: Your what?

MEERA: The third eye of Shiva.

SADIE: Who's Shiva?

MEERA: He's a God, who lives on a mountaintop.

SADIE: Is he blue like the others?

MEERA: Hanh! And in the middle of his eyebrows he has a third eye, which he mostly keeps shut, because when he opens it –

SADIE: What?

MEERA: My God!

SADIE: What? What?

MEERA: The world falls away.

SADIE: What do you mean?

MEERA: All the things, the small things fall away and he sees at once with the pure light of truth. That's why they call him Destroyer of the World.

SADIE: See, that's cool. That is very cool.

BARRY comes out of the toilet.

BARRY: I have to go now.

MEERA: Hanh!

BARRY: I have my other job to go to.

MEERA: Ok.

BARRY: But, just to let you know the toilet's still blocked. I know a fella I can get down, but that won't be till the morning now. So –

MEERA: It's only one that's blocked, isn't it?

BARRY: Aye.

MEERA: Ok.

BARRY: Just wanted to let you know, like.

BARRY goes.

SADIE: He's weird. We've been here for hours and all he talks about is the toilet.

MEERA: It's his job.

SADIE: I think it's an excuse.

MEERA: For what?

SADIE: To talk to you.

MEERA: For what reason does he want to talk to me?

ARJUN comes out.

ARJUN: Sadie, your tea's ready. So, you should eat it while it's hot.

SADIE: Ok.

SADIE goes in.

ARJUN: (*Astonished.*) What have you been saying to her?

MEERA: If you talk to her nicely, she listens.

ARJUN: No, if *you* talk nicely she listens.

He sits down and continues writing in his book.

MEERA: Writing, son?

ARJUN: Aha.

MEERA: You still do that?

ARJUN: When I can.

MEERA: Just like your father. Remember he locked himself in that study for hours on end – jotting, jotting, files and files.

ARJUN: Whatever happened to them?

MEERA: Binned.

ARJUN: You didn't!

MEERA: Gathering dust they were.

ARJUN: That was his life story.

MEERA: Relax. In the attic they are, with Mr Perky.

ARJUN: You put Mr Perky in the attic?

MEERA: Gathering dust he was.

ARJUN: He was my best friend.

MEERA: A bag of dust and mites is all he was, and who's got the energy to dust?

ARJUN: You tired?

MEERA: Hahn!

ARJUN: Have a lie down.

MEERA: No, no, we need to get going now. The vigils here are very popular.

ARJUN: You sure you're up to it?

MEERA: Of course. Even Sadie wants to come.

ARJUN: No. She's staying here.

MEERA: Why?

ARJUN: She's having blackouts.

MEERA: The doctor said, 'Not to worry.'

ARJUN: Bronagh is worried.

MEERA: Oh it's Bronwyn, is it?

ARJUN: (*Sharp.*) Her name's Bronagh ok? (*Beat.*) And you know Sadie used to have blackouts...you know...after.

MEERA: (*Beat.*) So it's just the two of us?

ARJUN: That's the thing...

MEERA: What?

ARJUN: I think I should be here with them.

MEERA: What?

ARJUN: I think I should.

Beat.

MEERA: Fine.

ARJUN: But, I'll take you there and pick you up.

MEERA: Don't worry about me, ok?

ARJUN: I'll order you a taxi.

MEERA: What are you a rich man now? Richard Branson?

ARJUN: Mum be reasonable.

MEERA: Reasonable bullshit!! Are you being reasonable? Is she?

ARJUN: She's worried about Sadie.

MEERA: Then let them stay. But you can come with me, can't you?

ARJUN: I told you I'll pick you up –

MEERA: No.

ARJUN: How will you get there?

MEERA: I'll fly.

ARJUN: Mum –

MEERA: If your father was here, this would never be happening.

ARJUN: What do you mean?

MEERA: He would have put her in her place.

ARJUN: You mean he would have lashed out.

MEERA: Perhaps that's what she needs – one rap across the teeth?

ARJUN: And what would that solve?

MEERA: It would shut her up at least.

ARJUN: Did it shut you up?

MEERA: Oh who cares! My life is over. Soon I will be dead. And maybe then you will think about me? Maybe then you will plant a tree in my honour. And under that tree maybe a flower will grow, and one day, maybe you will see that flower and maybe there will be tears in your eyes and maybe you will water that flower with your tears –

ARJUN: Maybe you'll shut up!

MEERA: What?!

ARJUN: I can't stand it when you go on like this.

MEERA: Then go! Get out of my sight! Piss off!

ARJUN: Is there any need for language like that?

MEERA: Piss off! Fuck off!

MEERA takes off her chuppal (Indian sandal.) and launches it at his head. It misses.

ARJUN: Mum –

With difficulty MEERA takes off her other chuppal and is about to throw it.

Calm down! Just –

There is a stand-off. MEERA drops her chuppal on the ground, and turns away leaning on the table, breathing heavily. ARJUN goes into the caravan. MEERA retrieves one of her chuppals, still breathing heavily. BARRY enters with a sign: CUBICLE NOT IN USE.

BARRY: I've made a sign for the toilet, Mrs.

MEERA continues to breathe heavily. She looks unsteady on her feet.

Are you alright there?

MEERA is still out of breath.

MEERA: I have a ventral wall defect.

BARRY: Can you not get a builder to sort that out?

MEERA: It's my heart idiot!

BARRY: Oh! God! Oh! I'll get you a glass of water.

BARRY goes, returning a few moments later with water, during which time MEERA sits still breathing heavily. She drinks.

MEERA: The valves in my heart don't work properly. Don't pump the blood well. That's why I breathing am like this. (*She drinks.*) Last year I collapsed in my house. Rushed to hospital. Then they discovered it. But, what can they do? Nothing. Just give me drugs and wait for the next one. The big one.

BARRY: You ok now?

MEERA: Yes. I thought you were going home.

27

BARRY: Not home Mrs. My other job.

MEERA: What's that?

BARRY: I help out in the bar of the hotel there.

MEERA: Won't you be late?

BARRY: No, it's not a job like that.

MEERA: What kind of job is it?

BARRY: I do it for the craic.

MEERA: The crack?

BARRY: The laugh. The company.

MEERA: You don't have a family to go to?

BARRY: No.

MEERA: Brothers? Sisters?

BARRY: I have a sister lives in Athlone.

MEERA: You see her?

BARRY: No.

MEERA: Just as well. Ungrateful bastards. You give them everything, they give you shit. Look at that one. I brought him up, cared for him. Now he is telling me to shut up. Because of her – who else? The problem is he can't stand up to her. The problem is anything she says he will do. Look, we were supposed to be going to vigil tonight –

BARRY: But her daughter's not well, Mrs.

MEERA: It's not about the daughter.

BARRY: Is it a lift you need?

MEERA: No, no, don't bother yourself.

BARRY: It's no bother, Mrs.

Beat.

MEERA: Actually, why not?! Why the hell not?!

BARRY: The car's just behind the office. Will I help you?

MEERA: No, I can walk.

BARRY: I'll help you.

MEERA: I can walk.

BARRY goes offstage. With difficulty MEERA gets up and follows. Just as she is moving offstage, ARJUN comes out of the caravan followed closely by BRONAGH.

ARJUN: Mum, where are you going?

MEERA: To the vigil.

ARJUN: Alone?

MEERA: No, with your father.

BRONAGH: We had a chat, Meera. He's going to come with you.

MEERA: I'm getting a lift now.

ARJUN: Who with?

MEERA: The janitor.

ARJUN: Is he going to bring you back?

MEERA: Don't worry about me ok?

ARJUN: What time does it wind up?

MEERA: Don't worry.

MEERA goes. ARJUN stands there worrying, wavering.

ARJUN: Should I go?

BRONAGH: She's got Barry with her now.

ARJUN: She's not well.

BRONAGH: She looks ok to me.

ARJUN: Was this a bad idea?

BRONAGH: What?

ARJUN: This whole caravan trip.

BRONAGH: You're fretting, Arjun.

ARJUN: Mum's always loved these places – Lourdes, Fatima.

BRONAGH: Stop fretting.

ARJUN: And seeing as it's on the way to Galway, I just thought –

BRONAGH: Relax.

ARJUN: I feel like my head's going to explode.

BRONAGH: Take a pill.

ARJUN: What does she do all day alone in that house in Beckenham?

BRONAGH: Hasn't she got hobbies?

ARJUN: Indians don't have hobbies.

BRONAGH: What?

ARJUN: Not her generation. It's all about the family – that's all there is.

BRONAGH: She's got a sister in India, hasn't she?

ARJUN: They don't speak.

BRONAGH: Perhaps they should start.

ARJUN: You want to send her to India now?

BRONAGH: If it's family she needs –

ARJUN: And what are we?

BRONAGH: What are you saying Arjun?

ARJUN: I don't know…

BRONAGH: You want her to come and live with us in Dublin?

ARJUN: She's my mother.

BRONAGH: She doesn't like me.

ARJUN: Of course she likes you.

BRONAGH: She won't even remember my name.

ARJUN: You're supposed to be making an effort here?

BRONAGH: Who spent all afternoon in that tiny kitchen being ordered about like a bleeding skivvy?

ARJUN: I know.

BRONAGH: And I'm here, aren't I? On holiday. Do you think I'd choose to come here –

ARJUN: Oh yeah, holiday! I forgot!

BRONAGH: What?

ARJUN: See the beach, see the shrine, see the shrink –

BRONAGH: And all in a fucking caravan.

ARJUN laughs.

It's not funny.

ARJUN can't stop laughing.

(*Catching his laughter.*) It's not. It's... (*They both can't stop laughing till they laugh themselves out. Beat.*) She's blacking out again, Arjun.

ARJUN: She's ok.

BRONAGH: It's only been a year, you know. Even adults who've been through things like that take years –

ARJUN: I know –

BRONAGH: And look what happened at school.

ARJUN: Kids, Bronagh.

BRONAGH: You know what started it, don't you? The other girl calling her a loony.

ARJUN: So?

BRONAGH: Not a slag or a gobshite, Arjun.

ARJUN: That doesn't mean –

BRONAGH: It's because she's withdrawn into herself. She's lost her friends.

ARJUN: She has friends. She was on the phone to Angelina this morning.

BRONAGH: That wasn't Angelina she was speaking to. It was Derbhle Kelly.

ARJUN: No.

BRONAGH: I heard it Arjun.

ARJUN: And you didn't say anything?

BRONAGH: When I can't even ask her to do the washing up without war?

ARJUN: I'll talk to her.

BRONAGH: And I was worried.

ARJUN: Ok I'll stand there and look supportive when you talk to her.

BRONAGH: Will you?

ARJUN: Yes.

BRONAGH: When?

ARJUN: Tomorrow morning. Before we head off.

Beat.

BRONAGH: I was here before, you know. Mam dragged me here just after Dad left. She was having a nervous breakdown at the time. Though no one talked about it. We ended up in confession. Why? I hadn't done anything. Even at that age, I thought this is all just nothing, just superstition. Making up sins and talking them into the ether. Then afterwards the two of us sat saying Hail Marys in the Chapel of Reconciliation, and she started sobbing and I put my hand on her arm, and she didn't even turn round. Just sat there, and never said a word. (*Beat.*) I want to be a better Mother than that.

ARJUN: You are. (*He kisses her forehead.*) I'm going to find Mum. I'll be back soon.

He goes.

The light fades.

SCENE 3

Middle of the night. The caravan site is in complete darkness and lit only by the dim camp lights. The set as before. SADIE comes round upstage corner of the caravan. She is smoking and holding a mobile phone to her ear.

SADIE: I have to whisper. I'm sneaking a fag. I have so got to cut down, but God I need this. (*She takes a drag.*) Just to say Greetings. The story so far: Mam's being a bitch, Arjun's running after her like a poodle, and I made a new friend. She's great like, really fantastic. I was going to write you a postcard, but my arm fell off, so I'm leaving you this message. Laters.

She hangs up. She has a drag on her fag. Then she hits recall and puts the phone back to her ear.

(*Pause.*) Me again. Forgot to say, was it you I saw with Noel O'Sullivan on Dame Street last Friday? I was on a bus and you were standing in the rain. I shouted from the bus, but you didn't turn round. Why didn't you turn round? I was

jumping up and down like trying to get yer attention. I was
like yer man outside Easons on O'Connell Street, yer man
with the pissy trousers, who dances like a mad thing. People
must have thought I was mad, but you didn't turn round.
(*Beat.*) Too interested in Noel, I bet. Noel eh?! The God of
Sex! Remember how we gave him the 'Most Promising Arse
In Jeans' award last year? Saying that he's not really my type.
I can see why you like him though. No, his brother Kieran
was always more my type. Hey would you get Noel to put a
word in? Drop my name into conversation, in passing like, see
what he says, or does, or the expression on his face. And don't
make it obvious like you did with Peter Hickey cos I couldn't
get rid of him then for a term and he'd a face like a gorilla on
heat. I'm relying on you now as my friend. My best friend.

*She hangs up. She has another drag on her fag. Then she hits recall
again, puts the phone back to her ear.*

(*Pause.*) Jesus Derbhle answerphones I hate them! I forgot to
say what happened this afternoon. I had this blackout thing.
It was mad: one minute I was there. The next I woke up in
bed with everyone round me, and Mam holding my hand
crying and a doctor there as well. Thing is she was there when
it happened, my friend. She's great, amazing. She listens to
everything I say and she's so beautiful. You'd love her. She's
there now. Waiting for me in the field. I have to go and see
her. Just thought I'd say a quick hello. (*Beat.*) Look, I know
you've been busy with stuff and that's why you haven't got
back to me, but when things calm down, you will call me,
won't you? And we'll hang out like we did before? (*She notices
something offstage. A light.*) That's her now. I have to go. I'll call
you again, but you know how it is with Mam. She hates me
calling you cos she knows I can talk to you. And last week she
said she'd throw me out of the house if she ever caught me
calling you again and I said, "Do it!" Cos when I'm gone, I'm
never coming back. Never! I'll be away Derbhle, away like
you. Just like you.

*SADIE goes offstage. The light gets brighter. We hear the dawn
chorus. Straight into:*

SCENE 4

Early hours of the morning. MEERA and BARRY come on from the direction of the shrine. MEERA looks exhausted: her breathing is shallow and fast. BARRY is helping her along.

BARRY: It's ok, Mrs. We're here now. We're home.

He helps her into a chair.

Are you ok now? Are you in pain?

MEERA: Yes.

BARRY: Where?

MEERA: Everywhere. I feel hot.

BARRY: Will I get you some water?

MEERA: No.

BARRY: A nice cool glass of water?

MEERA: (*Snaps.*) No, I said. Nothing.

Beat.

BARRY: Brandy?

MEERA: A small one.

BARRY pads off.

A small one though because normally I don't drink.

BARRY arrives back and presents her with a brandy miniature.

What's this?

BARRY: A small one.

MEERA: Where did you get it?

BARRY: I keep it in the office there.

MEERA: What for?

BARRY: Emergencies.

MEERA drinks her brandy down in one. She gets her breath back.

Better?

MEERA: I'm panicking.

BARRY: About what?

Beat.

BARRY cracks open a brandy for himself.

MEERA: You're having one?

BARRY: Aye.

MEERA: What for?

BARRY: Emergency.

He drinks.

MEERA: You like to drink, don't you?

BARRY: Aye.

MEERA: You were drinking this morning. I smelt it on your breath.

BARRY: I may have had a small one.

MEERA: (*Piercing.*) Who has a small one at seven o'clock in the morning?

BARRY: Did you enjoy the vigil Mrs?

MEERA: No.

BARRY: I thought it was peaceful.

MEERA: How do you know? Half asleep you were. Your head nodding like a dog's.

BARRY: I was drowsy is all.

MEERA: Then you should have gone home. Gone to bed. Who asked you to stay? You don't even believe in the Virgin anyway.

BARRY: So what?

MEERA: Then why are you working here?

BARRY: It's a job.

MEERA: Hut! Working here and saying that!

BARRY: Sure it's not even your religion Mrs.

MEERA: Who cares?

BARRY: You're a Hindi.

MEERA: A Hindu I am. Hindi is the language, idiot! And so, what? You call her Mary, we call her Parvati, or Durga or Devi? So what? It's the same thing – the Mother – because she cares like only a mother can care.

BARRY: Well, she never cared for me.

MEERA: How can you say that?

BARRY: Cos it's true.

MEERA: Perhaps she cares for you in ways you can't possibly imagine. Perhaps she's interceding for you in heaven right now.

BARRY: Big swinging knickers! Ways I can't possibly imagine! That was like when me Da used to hit me with a belt, he'd say, 'One day you'll thank me for this.' Well, I don't, and he's dead, and no comebacks now.

MEERA: Your father hit you with a belt?

BARRY: Yeah.

MEERA: Good! You deserved it.

BARRY: Ah shut up!

MEERA: (*Fierce.*) No you shut up! (*Tearful.*) Everyone's telling me to shut up today.

BARRY: …I'm only trying to help you Mrs.

MEERA: There's nothing you can do.

BARRY: About what?

MEERA: It doesn't matter.

BARRY: You can tell me Mrs.

MEERA: There's nothing you can do. Nothing anyone –

BARRY: Just spit it out will ya?

MEERA: I'm going to die.

   Beat.

BARRY: Sure, we're all going to die Mrs.

MEERA: Here! Tonight, maybe. I know it. I have dreamt it. I am with Sadie and we are walking in the field. She is playing, laughing. She brings me to the hollow of a tree and tells me to look inside, but the hollow is so dark. Then I am in the hollow, enclosed in the darkness, and Sadie, Arjun, all the ones are in another place. I can hear them laughing, talking, calling me, but I am suspended in this darkness. And slowly they go, their voices die, and there is silence, and I am forever frozen in this darkness. Alone… (*Beat.*) They say at my age you're supposed to be philosophical about it, but I'm not. Every night I wake up with my heart pounding against my ribs, my body drenched in sweat.

BARRY: Sure, it'll happen, when it happens.

MEERA: My husband went. Within a few months he was gone. Married forty years.

BARRY: But, you shouldn't dwell on it.

MEERA: Here speaks the sage!

BARRY: If you dwell on it, you'll not enjoy the time you have.

MEERA: St Patrick speaks!

BARRY: And cos he went like that, why should you? Sure if you look after yourself –

MEERA: (*Desperate.*) I'm dying – don't you understand? (*Beat.*) No you don't. You don't know what it's like to be sick, to be in hospital. And who are you to me anyway? Some drunkard! Some boosard! Go! Get out of my sight!

BARRY now gets up and walks towards the office.

Wait!

BARRY stops.

Please. I don't want to be alone.

BARRY comes back and sits down. He takes out another brandy miniature from his pocket and cracks it open. He drinks. They sit in silence for some moments.

BARRY: I do know what it's like to be sick Mrs. I was in hospital there myself.

MEERA: Why?

BARRY: I had a cyst.

MEERA: Where?

37

BARRY: Does it matter?

MEERA: You can't tell me half a story –

BARRY: It doesn't matter.

MEERA: I'm only asking.

BARRY: On my arse.

MEERA: Oh!

BARRY: You wanted to know.

MEERA: It's nothing to be ashamed of.

BARRY: Who said I was ashamed?

MEERA: You wouldn't tell me when I asked you.

BARRY is exasperated.

Was it serious?

BARRY: No. It was in and out the same day, but they had to put me under, see, and the thing was they told me I had to have someone waiting for me, to take me home like when I came round cos of the anaesthetic, and…well…that's what's started it.

MEERA: What?

BARRY: I didn't know who to ask. I didn't have anyone to ask.

MEERA: What about your sister?

BARRY: Ah no, sure she has problems of her own.

MEERA: So, what happened?

BARRY: I told them I had a friend waiting for me outside and I got the bus.

MEERA: Did you get home?

BARRY: Aye, but that's when it started –

MEERA: What?

BARRY: It's a feeling Mrs, all around you and inside you as well, every second of every day, everything you do, and some days it's bearable, but some days…the weekends were the worst. I'd just sit in the house feeling it swirl inside me Mrs. I remember this one weekend it was fierce. I couldn't think what to do with myself. So, I grabbed a paper that was lying there on the table, one of those free rags, and there was an advertisement for a fishing shop in Charlestown. 'That's it!,' I thought, 'I'll take up fishing.' I had to do something Mrs. I thought at least if I did that, I would be busy, get my mind off things. So, I got the bus. I remember it was one of those bright October mornings the sun streaming through the windows of the bus and I felt ok Mrs. No, I felt good. I kept thinking of myself on one of those big American lakes, just me in my little rowboat, fishing. But, when I got there, it had closed down. Gone out of business like. Must have been an old paper I was reading. So, I walked home and it started to rain, and I walked in the rain, and I thought: 'Wherever you go, grey clouds hover over you.' They're there now Mrs, you can't see them cos it's dark, but they're never far off, and I thought…I thought…

MEERA: What?

BARRY: I'd be better off dead than living like that. So, I went into the kitchen, and I got a knife, and I put it against my wrist.

MEERA: No!

BARRY: And I sat there all through the evening, and into the night –

MEERA: And what happened?

BARRY: I couldn't do it Mrs. I couldn't even do that.

MEERA: Thank God.

BARRY: But, I learned something that night.

MEERA: What?

BARRY: When you're sad, you think the world owes you happiness, and the sadder you are, the happier you think you will be one day, but that's not true. No one owes you anything, and most times no one even knows what you're going through, or cares and no one's listening Mrs. No one. Not even God.

MEERA: Someone is listening.

BARRY: Who?

MEERA: Me. (*Beat.*) So, the feeling, did it go away?

BARRY: Sure, they're never far off – those clouds.

MEERA: I know.

BARRY: Do you?

MEERA: I lived alone for forty years.

BARRY: But, you were married.

MEERA: He was going to England. I went with him. That was it.

BARRY: It wasn't a love marriage?

MEERA: What is love? Love is in the movies only. Not here. Not for me. But, I did feel for him at the end. Arre such a strong man drifting in and out, on drugs, in pain. But, sometimes there were moments in between when he'd know, when he'd hold my hand, when he'd say: 'Not yet, Meera. I'm not ready yet.' Arre what could I do? What can anyone...

BARRY: It's ok Mrs. It's ok.

Beat.

MEERA: Thank you.

BARRY: No, thank you.

MEERA: For what?

BARRY: For talking to me Mrs. Most people think I'm just a strange man with a beard.

She laughs.

MEERA: Call me Meera.

BARRY: Sweet dreams, Meera. I'm Barry.

There is a moment between them, broken by a burst of laughter. Suddenly they become aware of a figure at the edge of the stage, framed in the darkness.

MEERA: Who's that?

The figure does not respond.

Arre! Who's there?

SADIE steps out of the shadows. She is beaming.

Darling you scared me! Where have you come from?

SADIE: The field.

MEERA: What were you doing in the field at this time of night?

SADIE: I've been with my friend.

MEERA: She should be in bed. So should you.

SADIE: She'll not go to bed, Meera.

MEERA: She'll get terrible bags under her eyes.

This sets SADIE off laughing again.

Arre?

BARRY: Where's your mam?

SADIE: Asleep.

BARRY: Does she know you're awake?

SADIE: Will you come with me Meera? Come into the field.

MEERA: It's too late darling.

SADIE: I want you to meet her.

MEERA: Who is she?

SADIE: It's a mystery.

BARRY: Sure, the only mystery's why you're not tucked up.

SADIE: Please come, Meera.

MEERA: Why now?

SADIE: She waiting for us by the hollow of the tree.

MEERA: What?

SADIE: ...and it's like you said – she makes the world fall away.

MEERA: What?

SADIE: She does Meera. She does.

Beat.

MEERA: Ok I'll come.

BARRY: Meera –

MEERA: It's ok, Barry. Let me go –

BARRY: But Meera –

MEERA: I have to do this Barry. I have to go.

SADIE helps MEERA into the field, leaving BARRY on stage.
Blackout.

SCENE 5

Morning. 6 am. ARJUN is at the table scribbling in his notebook. BRONAGH comes out of the caravan looking agitated.

ARJUN: Why don't you sit down?

BRONAGH: No.

ARJUN: They've only gone for a walk.

BRONAGH: Your Mother can't walk. Six o'clock in the morning they're off in the field!

ARJUN: Chill.

BRONAGH: (*Agitated.*) I AM CHILLED.

BARRY comes out of the office with two mugs of tea. He too seems a little preoccupied.

BARRY: There you go.

ARJUN: Thanks.

BARRY: Did yous want sugar?

ARJUN/BRONAGH: No.

BARRY: Good. Cos I have none.

Beat.

The toilet's still blocked.

ARJUN: Yeah.

BARRY: But, you'll be away. Galway! You'll like that now. And it's an easy enough drive, just take the N road through Tuam.

BRONAGH: We know.

BARRY: I've never been to Tuam, would you believe it? Living here all these years. I've been through it like, but I've never stopped and had a look around.

Beat.

BRONAGH: How can they go for a walk at six o'clock in the morning?

BARRY: She was laughing and joking about her friend.

BRONAGH: Who is this friend?

BARRY: I reckon it could be one of the traveller's children – they sometimes park up there in the field.

BRONAGH: I need a fag. Have you got one Barry?

BARRY: I've got a rolly.

BRONAGH: That will do.

ARJUN: You've given up.

BRONAGH: I'm starting again. (*BRONAGH sits.*) And I have had the worst night's sleep.

ARJUN: I haven't slept.

BRONAGH: I'll be driving then.

ARJUN: I can drive.

BRONAGH: And kill us all? (*Beat.*) What kept you anyway?

ARJUN: What?

BRONAGH: 'Back soon,' you said.

ARJUN: I got talking.

BRONAGH: To who?

ARJUN: Someone.

BRONAGH: About what?

ARJUN: Everything.

BRONAGH: What are you going on about Arjun?

ARJUN: Last night I needed to talk to someone.

BRONAGH: You should have gone to confession, Arjun.

ARJUN: I did.

BRONAGH: What? You're a Hindu.

ARJUN: Does it matter?

BRONAGH: So, you talked to some priest you don't even know?

ARJUN: Yes.

BRONAGH: About what?

ARJUN: It doesn't matter.

BRONAGH: About us?

ARJUN: No

BRONAGH: What then?

ARJUN: I talked about my job. About how I fell into it, how on
    Sunday nights, I get this feeling in the pit of my stomach.

BRONAGH: And, what did he say?

ARJUN: He gave me some prayers to say.

BRONAGH: Fucking brilliant!

ARJUN: At least he listened to me.

BRONAGH: What the fuck is that supposed to mean?

BARRY: I think I'll go and check the toilet now.

BARRY goes into the toilet.

BRONAGH: So, did you say your Hail Marys?

ARJUN: I just sat there in the Apparition Chapel with all the rest of
    them. My mind went blank, and suddenly I sensed something
    I can't articulate. So big, I just sensed the edge of it, the edge
    of the biggest, greatest thing and I knew I had to go up to the
    top of that hill and watch the sunrise, so I walked up to the top
    of that hill and sat there for two hours, possibly more. All I
    could feel was the air on my face, and the intense moment and
    when it came and it was magnificent, it's rays shot through
    me, and that's when I heard the voice.

BRONAGH: Oh God!

ARJUN: No, it wasn't him, I don't think so anyway.

BRONAGH: Who was it then?

ARJUN: It was me. My own voice. Not Mum or you or anyone
    else, free of stress, of useless thoughts, and that's when I knew
    it, what I have to do, why I was put here on this Earth.

BRONAGH: What are you talking about?

ARJUN: I have a story to tell, Bronagh.

BRONAGH: What story?

ARJUN: My father's story.

BRONAGH: What?

ARJUN: How he left a distant land, thousands of miles away to
    make his life in England and not just his story, but the story

a thousand others leaving in search of a better life, and a title even came to me: 'Diaspora'.

BRONAGH: Ok.

ARJUN: I'm a writer Bronagh. I need to write this.

BRONAGH: To sleep is what you need.

ARJUN: I've never felt more sure of anything.

BRONAGH: Ok. Ok.

ARJUN: But, it will take time and work. So, I phoned the office.

BRONAGH: What?

ARJUN: I phoned Phil. I only got his answerphone.

BRONAGH: Why?

ARJUN: I quit.

BRONAGH: You quit?

ARJUN: I'm not wasting another second in that place.

BRONAGH: You quit?!

ARJUN: Perhaps I should have talked to you first –

BRONAGH: Perhaps?!

ARJUN: …but, up there on that hill it was all so clear to me.

BRONAGH: Phone him back, tell him you were stressed.

ARJUN: No.

BRONAGH: You can't just quit Arjun.

ARJUN: Why not?

BRONAGH: We're buying a house.

ARJUN: This is going to work for us.

BRONAGH: If you phone him now –

ARJUN: No.

BRONAGH: Look, you're stressed. You need a holiday. A proper break, and I do listen to you. I listened to what you said last night about your mother and perhaps when the house is up and running, she could come and stay with us for a while and we'll see, ok? So, stop fretting and call Phil –

ARJUN: No.

BRONAGH: Call him.

ARJUN: No.

BRONAGH: What's got into you?

ARJUN: Maybe it's this place Bronagh. Maybe we were brought here for a reason.

BRONAGH: Nothing brought us here, Arjun. We drove.

BARRY comes out of the toilets. An awkward moment.

BARRY: So, yous are off to Galway? That's a nice place. If there's one place I like it's Galway, and it's an easy enough drive just take the main road through Tuam. I have never been to Tuam would you believe it? All these years. I've been through it like, in the car, but I've never stopped, and had a walk around (*Beat.*) So, will you be coming back this way, do you think?

BRONAGH: No. I can't stand this place.

ARJUN: Bronagh!

BRONAGH: It's a shithole.

ARJUN: The guy works here Bronagh.

BARRY: It's ok.

ARJUN: No, it's not ok. You can't say that.

BRONAGH: Why not?

ARJUN: It an important place for some people.

BRONAGH: It's a dump, an old, grey, concrete dump. I thought that the first time I came here and it hasn't changed. It's the Catholic church all over. Everything I grew up with. I mean what's spiritual about this place? Tell me? The apparition? Who believes that? Who even cares? It's a joke. A big, fucking laugh. I was in the shrine yesterday, I saw this booklet, 'Why go to Mass?' Good question, I thought. Don't get me wrong, I'm not saying we didn't need it once, when we were dirt poor, and had nothing else. Then it gave us something, a dream of something. I mean that's all the apparition was: a starving beggar seeing a meal there in front of him, cos they were starving those people who saw it, and they needed a dream, but we don't live in the dirt like they did, and we've outgrown this place with its tack and tradition. It doesn't serve us. We are serving it. Keeping it alive like some ancient, dying relative –

ARJUN: What about those people in the Apparition chapel?

BRONAGH: They're clinging on, Arjun.

ARJUN: They believe.

BRONAGH: Who believes Arjun? Not the people we know. They're not in church on Sunday. They're at the gym, or the shops or away for the weekend, and the truth is: there won't even be churches in a hundred years time. It doesn't matter how they market themselves. Those places are for weddings and funerals now.

SADIE walks on.

BARRY: Bingo!

BRONAGH: Where have you been?

SADIE: In the field with Meera.

BRONAGH: Doing what?

SADIE: I took her to see my friend.

BRONAGH: What friend? Which friend?

SADIE: The girl.

BRONAGH: Which girl?

SADIE: I don't know her name.

BRONAGH: Great friend –

SADIE: Something happened…

BRONAGH: What?

SADIE: (*Starting to cry.*) Something happened…to Meera.

BARRY: What happened?

SADIE is crying now.

SADIE: I…I don't know.…I…didn't do it…I…

ARJUN: Sadie, where's Mum? Where is she?

MEERA: Here.

MEERA walks on easily without her crutch. She kneels down, embraces SADIE.

ARJUN: Mum?… You're walking.

BRONAGH: What's going on? What the fuck is going on?

MEERA: It's ok Bronagh. Thank God. You have an angel here.

Blackout.

Act Two

SCENE 1

Later, same day. 12 pm. The caravan as before, except now MEERA's crutch leans against the side of it, and there are cards and little gifts scattered around, including a luminous statue of Padre Pio. Offstage noise suggests the buzz of people, and somewhere a group of people are singing Ave Maria – the hymn of Lourdes version – we first heard played on the ornament in Act One. This competes with music emanating from the toilets – Zorba the Greek. ARJUN sits at the table staring into a laptop. He writes a sentence. He deletes it immediately. The offstage singers get through almost three verses in harmony, while Zorba the Greek gets more frenetic.

ARJUN: (*Screams.*) Shut up!

Ave Maria stops. BARRY comes of the toilet out holding a plunger.

BARRY: What? What?

ARJUN: The music.

BARRY: Sorry.

BARRY goes in and lowers the volume. He returns.

I put it on sometimes when I'm working. I went on holiday to Crete. Don't go on many holidays. It reminds me. (*Beat.*) Are you enjoying your holiday?

ARJUN: Yes.

BARRY: Next stop: Galway!

ARJUN: Yes.

BARRY: You'll like that now, you'll enjoy that. Oh yes. And it's a nice day for a drive, don't you think?

ARJUN: Sorry?

BARRY: Nice day for driving.

ARJUN: Yes.

BARRY: Or walking. (*Beat.*) Or a boat ride. You could take the boat to Inishmor. Have you been to Inishmor?

ARJUN: No.

BARRY: That's what you should do. You should take the boat to Inishmor.

ARJUN: Barry, I'm trying to work.

BARRY: Oh sorry! (*Beat.*) What page you on now?

ARJUN: One.

BARRY: Still?

ARJUN: I keep writing then deleting the same sentence.

BARRY: Oh dear.

ARJUN: Must be this computer. I was fine with pen and ink.

BARRY: Have you a blockage?

ARJUN: What?

BARRY: I mean…what do they call it?

ARJUN: Writer's block? I hope not Barry. I've just started.

BARRY: Ah you'll be fine. It's just the beginning, isn't it? Like jumping into a swimming pool. I hate jumping into swimming pools. All cold and wet. An awful combination that. And before ever I do see? I always have to say to myself, 'Jump Barry! Jump!' You should give it a try, maybe. Jump! (*Louder.*) Go on! Jump!

ARJUN doesn't react.

Cos what is it they say: 'A journey of a thousand miles begins with one step?'

ARJUN: Yeah.

BARRY: And what is it they say, 'We've all go a book inside of us.'

ARJUN: Yeah. Yeah.

BARRY: Mind you they also say you can't have your cake and eat it. I've never understood that. If you have a cake – why can't you eat it? It's your cake after all…

ARJUN puts his head in his hands.

Sorry. I'm talking shite now. Talking for the sake of talking, ever since last night, ever since what happened. I can't stop talking,

Beat.

Is it hard writing books?

ARJUN: (*Annoyed.*) I don't know.

BARRY: Only we never had books in our house. The fella next door had books, a retired schoolteacher he was. That one he lent me. That racy book from England. About the Lady of the Manor falling for a servant – dirty words in it, and all.

ARJUN: Lady Chatterly's Lover?

BARRY: Em…no, 'My Mistress Desires' it was called. A great book. A story of forbidden love. Oh yeah a great book that was. And to write it. I wouldn't know where to start. Sure, I have stories in my head like, but to write them down –

The phone rings. BARRY goes off into the office. ARJUN stares in the laptop. He types a sentence. Then deletes it immediately. BRONAGH comes out of the caravan.

BRONAGH: Are you packing away?

ARJUN: Does it look like it?

BRONAGH: Three o'clock we have to be there.

ARJUN: I know.

BRONAGH: And where's your mother?

ARJUN: She's talking to Heather next door.

BRONAGH: What about?

ARJUN: What am I psychic?

BRONAGH: You know they've been calling here, don't you?

ARJUN: Who?

BRONAGH: Religious nuts.

ARJUN: People are interested, Bronagh.

BRONAGH: Oh who cares, we're out of here anyway. Just need to get on the road.

ARJUN: What's the rush?

BRONAGH: We still have to find the place, Arjun.

ARJUN: Ok.

BRONAGH: And I don't suppose you've called Phil yet?

ARJUN: No.

BRONAGH: Have you thought about it at least?

ARJUN: Yes.

BRONAGH: I think you should call him, Arjun.

ARJUN: It's Saturday – he won't be there.

BRONAGH: It's important, Arjun.

ARJUN: (*Referring to his work.*) So is this. (*Beat.*) Anyway do you always listen to me?

BRONAGH: When it's important –

ARJUN: So, why are we rushing off to Galway?

BRONAGH: What are you talking about? We planned it.

ARJUN: We don't have to stick to the plan.

BRONAGH: She hallucinating, she's blacking out.

ARJUN: Yeah, but apart from that, she's fine.

BRONAGH: What the fuck are you on?

BARRY comes out of the office.

BARRY: Sorry, to interrupt. Em…there's a call for you.

BRONAGH: Who?

BARRY: Some fella asking after the girl.

BRONAGH: Who?

BARRY: Some fella.

BRONAGH: See, this is what I mean. This is your mother shouting her mouth off.

ARJUN: Tell him she's fine.

BRONAGH: Tell him it's none of his fucking business!

ARJUN: Bronagh –

BRONAGH: Tell him if he rings again, I will find him and stick the telephone up his –

ARJUN: Bronagh!

BARRY: I'll just say you're busy.

BARRY goes off.

ARJUN: What's got into you?

BRONAGH: We need to get on the road Arjun.

BRONAGH goes off into the caravan, closing the door firmly. ARJUN closes his computer. BARRY comes back on.

ARJUN: Sorry about that.

BARRY: People get stressed when these things happen.

ARJUN: It's happened before?

BARRY: Sure, we're a miracle site, we're in the business. Don't get me wrong now. We're not Lourdes or Medugorge, where miracles are ten a penny or so they say, but you do get the odd thing here.

ARJUN: Yeah? When was the last one?

BARRY: Oh it was some years ago now, nine or ten at least. The last big thing.

ARJUN: What happened?

BARRY: Some women with MS, and she was very sick, in a wheelchair like, and they wheeled her into the Apparition chapel, and they say she walked out like.

ARJUN: Really?

BARRY: So they say.

ARJUN: Wow!

BARRY: Oh yeah.

ARJUN: Did you see it?

BARRY: No, I didn't see it.

ARJUN: And what happened to her?

BARRY: She moved to Canada, I believe.

ARJUN: And she's cured?

BARRY: So they say.

ARJUN: Amazing.

BARRY: Oh there are a fair few stories like that. Sure, in the years just after the Apparition, didn't they all use to leave their crutches leaning against the wall where she appeared and go walking off? Hundreds of crutches there were against that wall.

ARJUN: And was it… (*Signifies the Virgin.*) HER you think?

BARRY: I don't know.

ARJUN: How do you explain it then?

BARRY: Sure, what are asking me for? I have trouble explaining how to use the ansaphone in the office there.

They laugh. MEERA arrives. She is like a different person – lighter, freer, more playful.

MEERA: What's funny?

ARJUN: Nothing.

MEERA: Tell me, no?

ARJUN: Said your goodbyes?

MEERA: Everyone's begging me to stay.

ARJUN: We can't. We have to be in Galway.

MEERA: We can't spend one more night here?

ARJUN: No.

MEERA: Such nice places Heather was telling me of. What was the name of that one? Knocknacree – you know it Barry?

BARRY: Oh yeah.

MEERA: It's a big pile of stones, under which they say a queen lies buried.

BARRY: Oh yeah. It's magical.

MEERA: Let's go for a daytrip, Arjun.

ARJUN: No.

MEERA: Such a nice day it is. No clouds in the sky.

ARJUN: We have to be in Galway.

MEERA: Galway! Galway! Why do we have to be in Galway?

ARJUN: We don't have to be in Galway.

MEERA: You just said –

ARJUN: I meant –

MEERA: What is it, Arjun? What's going on?

ARJUN: (*Rubbing his nose.*) Nothing's going on.

MEERA: You know when you're lying Arjun, you rub your nose.

He stops rubbing his nose.

Ever since you were a little boy you've done that

He starts rubbing the back of his head.

Or the back of your head, you rub.

ARJUN: You're making self-conscious now.

MEERA: Speak.

Beat.

ARJUN: …there's someone in Galway we need to see.

MEERA: Who?

ARJUN: A professional.

MEERA: Who?

ARJUN: A psychiatrist.

MEERA: Are you depressed?

ARJUN: For Sadie.

MEERA: What? (*Beat.*) When was this arranged?

ARJUN: Some time ago.

MEERA: So, that's why we're going to Galway?

ARJUN: And to have a holiday of course. Look, he's supposed to be amazing this guy.

MEERA: But, you think the girl needs a psychiatrist?

ARJUN: (*Rubbing his nose.*) Yes.

MEERA: You're rubbing your nose again.

ARJUN: She needs to talk to someone.

MEERA: It's her, isn't it? It's Bronagh.

ARJUN: (*Rubbing his nose.*) No.

MEERA: Again you're rubbing your nose.

ARJUN: Will you cut it out.

MEERA: And what about what Sadie wants? What if the Virgin is there again?

ARJUN: We don't know it was the Virgin.

MEERA: I do. I know.

ARJUN: You didn't actually see anything.

MEERA: But, something I felt. A force, a power beyond belief, coming from the heart of that little girl, and it was when she put her hand here, on my heart, it was like a million volts shooting through me, waking me, bringing me back to life, and suddenly I could breathe, suddenly my legs had strength to carry me.

ARJUN: We're leaving in an hour ok?

MEERA: You can't ask her if we can stay even one night?

ARJUN: Get your stuff together.

MEERA: You're can't even ask?

ARJUN goes into the caravan.

BARRY: I understand you went to see the doctor here?

MEERA: Yes.

BARRY: And he said there was an improvement with your heart?

MEERA: Yes.

BARRY: Did he think it was a miracle?

MEERA: A miracle he couldn't declare. Not until he had done more tests, but a marvel he said it was.

BARRY: What's that?

MEERA: Like a miracle. Only smaller.

BARRY: A small miracle. I like that.

MEERA: I want to go to Knocknacree.

BARRY: Shame it's so far. (*Beat.*) There are closer places of course.

MEERA: Yes?

BARRY: Depends what you're after.

MEERA: Somewhere nice to walk, a river, a lake.

BARRY: There's the Munnin Lake.

MEERA: What's that?

BARRY: It's a lake. Near here.

MEERA: Is it nice?

BARRY: It is aye.

MEERA: Is it magical?

BARRY: Em… I wouldn't go that far, but it's only a short drive. I mean you could take the bus, but to drive would be better cos the buses aren't great, and sure you could be there and back in an hour.

MEERA: Will you drive me Barry?

BARRY: When?

MEERA: Now.

BARRY: (*Referring to the caravan.*) But, what about these?

MEERA: You said we could be there and back in an hour.

BARRY: But –

MEERA: You don't want to take me?

BARRY: No, I do, Meera. I really do –

MEERA: Then go! Start the car!

BARRY: Just like that?

MEERA: Why not? I'll leave a note. Go!

BARRY: You're class Meera! You're mad!

BARRY goes offstage. MEERA takes ARJUN's pen and scribbles a note on his notebook. She tears the page out and leaves it on top of his computer. Then she follows BARRY offstage.

The lights go down.

SCENE 2

6 pm. The caravan as before. Inside the caravan ARJUN and BRONAGH are in the midst of heated discussion. SADIE is on her own outside, her mobile phone to her ear.

SADIE: Hi, it me. It's Saturday night. I'm still here. What's everyone doing tonight? Wishing they were somewhere else. That's what most people do on Saturday nights. Do you reckon yer man outside Eason's still dancing? Or is he packed up for the day and sitting in some alleyway relaxing in his pissy trousers? 'Ah! The high life!' Sure, why does he dance anyway? Is he mad or something? (*Beat.*) What are you up to? Noel taking you out? The flicks? Are yous two an item then? Cos it's cool. I'm cool with that. I like Noel. He's mad, but. Remember that day he drove us up to Bray in his brother's car? That was mad, wasn't it? Remember yer woman shouting at us for standing outside her flat? To keep out of the rain like. Jesus! Some people are so uptight. Ok, it didn't help Noel calling her a fat whore, but that was in the heat of the moment and hadn't she just called us crackheads? But we laughed that day, didn't we? D'ya remember? (*Laughing.*) Dya remember that doorknocker looked like arse cheeks? And Noel pulling mad faces to freak yer one out? I'm near wetting myself just thinking about it. And then yer one going in to call the police. And you scarpering? Why did you do that? Hey did I ever tell you what Noel did that night after you ran? He pissed. Swear to God, he got dick out in front of me and pissed on her doorstep. It was awesome. What he did, I mean. Not his dick. Though that wasn't bad. Decent I'd say. More than decent. I don't fancy him though. He's not my type –

The door of the caravan opens and ARJUN emerges.

SADIE: Got to go. Got to go. (*She hangs up.*)

ARJUN: (*To BRONAGH inside.*) Look –

BRONAGH: Leave a message.

ARJUN: I'm busy. I'm working.

BRONAGH: Just walk away then you fuck!

He closes the door quite hard and comes down the steps.

SADIE: All good?

ARJUN: Yes.

He sits down and reads his work, and continues to type.

SADIE: Are you not finished yet?

ARJUN: Don't you start.

SADIE: You said you'd get me a burger.

ARJUN: I need to finish this.

SADIE: You said that an hour ago. What page you on?

ARJUN: Fifteen.

SADIE: That's loads, Arjun. That's enough for today.

ARJUN: It's just the beginning.

SADIE: How can it be? It's longer than the longest thing I ever wrote, which was my project about windows. Fourteen pages about windows? In the end, I wanted to jump out the frigging window!

ARJUN: You're talking to me, Sadie. When you talk to me I can't write…

The next two lines can be spoken over each other.

SADIE: My stomach is digesting itself.

ARJUN: …and while I can't write, I can't finish writing, can I?

SADIE: I'm feeling a bit faint actually… I'm feeling…

SADIE totters and falls to her knees then on the ground. She lies there for several moments, while ARJUN continues typing.

Arjun!

ARJUN continues to type.

I've fainted.

ARJUN continues to type.

Don't you even care?

ARJUN: You shouldn't joke about those things.

SADIE: Why not?

ARJUN: With your recent history?

SADIE: That wasn't fainting.

ARJUN: What was it then?

SADIE: Dunno.

Beat.

ARJUN: Was it something to do with the girl?

SADIE: S'pose.

ARJUN: What does she look like? The girl?

SADIE: Nothing special.

ARJUN: Is she like surrounded by light?

SADIE: Yes, and she floats on a cloud.

ARJUN: Really?

SADIE: No. She's normal.

ARJUN: What do you mean 'normal'?

SADIE: Like you or me.

ARJUN: What like in modern clothes?

SADIE: Yes.

ARJUN: It's not the Virgin then, is it?

SADIE: Dunno. Heather said when she comes, she comes in all
different shapes and sizes cos she knows what you need her to
be. Sometimes, she's like a woman draped in stars, but other
times she's just a girl – like she was with St Bernadette.

ARJUN: So, it is the Virgin?

SADIE: Dunno.

ARJUN: Why don't you ask her?

SADIE: I will when I see her next.

ARJUN: When will that be?

SADIE: Dunno. She'll call me.

ARJUN: Do you talk to her?

SADIE: Yeah.

ARJUN: About what?

SADIE: What is this twenty questions?

ARJUN: I'm just interested.

SADIE: Loads of things, but sometimes we don't talk at all cos it's
like with your best friend right? You don't have to talk. Me
and Derbhle were like that. Sometimes we'd just sit there and
say nothing. Have you ever had that with anyone?

ARJUN: Your mum. When she's asleep.

SADIE: Stop kidding about and finish your story. What's it about
anyway?

ARJUN: Nothing.

SADIE: What do you mean nothing?

ARJUN: It doesn't matter.

SADIE: Isn't it about Indian people coming over to England?

ARJUN: No.

SADIE: Mam said it was.

ARJUN: It isn't.

SADIE: What's it about then?

ARJUN: It's something new, an idea that came to me.

SADIE: About what?

ARJUN just keeps typing.

I could find out you know. I could look inside your mind.

ARJUN: Aha.

SADIE: I have the power Arjun. It may cause brain damage, but –

ARJUN keeps typing

I'm serious Arjun, not about the brain damage, but I can do it.

ARJUN: Aha.

ARJUN continues to type. SADIE stands to the side of him, composing herself, she extends one arm towards his head – her hand hovering above. ARJUN's head drops. He collapses in his chair, and lies limp.

SADIE: (*Scared.*) Arjun! Arjun!

Suddenly ARJUN gets up and roars at her, scaring her out of her wits.

I hate you ya Bollox!

ARJUN: Got you though.

SADIE: (*Diving on him.*) I'll get you! I'll fucking deck ya!

They fight. The noise brings BRONAGH out of the caravan.

BRONAGH: What the hell is going on?

They stop immediately.

ARJUN: We're just playing.

BRONAGH: Don't! If we're stuck here another night, let's try not to piss the neighbours off.

SADIE slopes off towards the toilets.

And where are you going?

SADIE: The jacks – is that ok?

SADIE heads into the toilet.

BRONAGH: I managed to get him on the phone. Do you want to know what he said?

ARJUN stops typing and looks at her.

He'll see her tomorrow.

ARJUN: Good.

BRONAGH: He doesn't usually see people on Sundays. I had to beg.

ARJUN continues to type

Your mother has a lot to answer for.

ARJUN: She didn't think –

BRONAGH: Oh she knew exactly what she was doing!

ARJUN: You always have to think the worst of her.

BRONAGH: What am I supposed to think?

ARJUN: It's just one more night –

BRONAGH: Well, in the morning, we're out of here.

ARJUN: I'm on your side, Bronagh.

BRONAGH: Prove it.

ARJUN: How?

BRONAGH: Turn the computer off.

ARJUN: I'm on a roll Bronagh.

BRONAGH: Step away from the masterpiece.

ARJUN: (*He turns it off, closes it.*) Ok, I'm turning it off. Now what?

BRONAGH: Call Phil.

ARJUN: No.

BRONAGH: Why not?

ARJUN: I'm not happy working there.

BRONAGH: Do you think I go in singing every day?

ARJUN: This is my work now.

BRONAGH: Work? (*She laughs.*) Do you know how many writers make a living?

ARJUN: It'll work out.

BRONAGH: It was worked out already.

ARJUN: Trust me.

BRONAGH: Like you trusted me when you didn't even consult me about this?

ARJUN: I need you to trust me.

BRONAGH: No.

ARJUN: What do you mean, 'No'?

BRONAGH: I didn't buy into this Arjun.

Beat.

ARJUN: You know what your problem is: you don't believe in anything.

BRONAGH: And you believe in everything like a little boy, who's come out of the cinema, thinking the film's real. But, it's not. Give it fifteen minutes and you'll realise that (*Beat.*) What are you looking for? Something to make your life amazing, to give it higher meaning. What was it last month? Meditation, before that – yoga – that was it yoga was going to change your life forever. Did it? We're buying a house on Vernon Street, Arjun. We're spending eight hundred and fifty thousand Euro –

A noise from the toilet. A voice. A laugh.

What was that?

ARJUN: What?

BRONAGH: She's talking in there.

ARJUN: Relax.

BRONAGH: She's on the mobile I bet.

ARJUN: Leave her.

BRONAGH: Sadie!

ARJUN: Will you just give it a rest? (*Beat.*) Look, I said I'd get her a burger.

BRONAGH: That'll be packed with goodness.

ARJUN: It's not going to kill her.

BRONAGH: No.

ARJUN: What about you? What do you want?

BRONAGH: Since when was that your concern?

ARJUN: From the chippy, I mean.

BRONAGH: Ask them if they've got eight hundred and fifty thousand Euro to spare.

BRONAGH goes into the caravan. ARJUN starts to put away his stuff. After some moments SADIE comes out of the toilets. She sits at the table.

SADIE: Arjun.

ARJUN: Yes.

SADIE: I'm feeling a bit…

She walks towards the field, engrossed.

ARJUN: Ok! You've done that joke, Sadie.

SADIE begins to weep.

Sadie –

She continues to walk towards the field, weeping, engrossed in some other thing. ARJUN approaches her.

Sadie –

SADIE: She's in the field, Arjun. She's calling me into the field.

ARJUN: What? Now?

SADIE: I have to see her.

ARJUN: I'm not sure your mum would agree.

SADIE: Please Arjun. She's calling me.

ARJUN: (*Putting a hand on her shoulder.*) No

SADIE: Please.

Fade out.

SCENE 3

9 pm and the caravan park is lit by dim camp lights. The set as before except on the grass is a stereo playing a Hindi film song at low volume. BRONAGH comes out of the caravan. Clocks it.

BRONAGH: Hello?

She follows the stereo's extension lead offstage. A beat.

(*Offstage.*) Oh dear God!

BRONAGH walks briskly back onstage, keeping her back towards the office she takes a cigarette from a packet, lights it and takes a pull. After a few moments, BARRY follows her on doing up his trousers.

BARRY: I'm sorry.

BRONAGH: It's ok.

BARRY: I should have closed the door.

BRONAGH: Yes.

BARRY: We didn't realise –

BRONAGH: Yes.

MEERA comes on tucking in her sari at the waist.

MEERA: Bronagh hi!

BRONAGH: Hi.

MEERA: We didn't hear you Bronagh. We didn't see you.

BRONAGH: Well, I saw you.

Beat. BRONAGH takes several pulls on her cigarette.

MEERA: Bronagh! You're smoking.

BRONAGH: That's nothing compared to what you were doing.

MEERA: We were at the lake.

BRONAGH: I know.

MEERA: We had a lovely time, didn't we Barry?

BARRY: We did, aye.

BRONAGH: Good.

MEERA: You're angry.

BRONAGH: What do you expect?

65

BARRY: It was my fault –

MEERA: No, it was me. I just fancied a ride.

BRONAGH: Well, you got that.

MEERA: Where's the others?

BRONAGH: You tell me.

BARRY: They're not with you?

BRONAGH: They went to get a burger. Three hours ago that was.

MEERA: Fast food I call that.

BRONAGH: I'm glad you find this funny –

MEERA: What you need is a drink.

BRONAGH: No.

MEERA: Have a drink. We had one earlier, or was it two?

BRONAGH: I don't want one, I said. (*Beat.*) The same goes for your false friendship.

MEERA: I don't want to fight with you Bronagh.

BRONAGH: Now she says it.

MEERA: I don't want to fight with anyone anymore.

BRONAGH: What's this? Saint Meera all of a sudden?

MEERA: I'm no Saint.

BRONAGH: I know that, but no one else around here seems to. Ever since what happened in that field, they think you're great! Divine – St Meera of fucking the Caravan Park.

The noise of an offstage crowd. ARJUN comes on.

A miracle! (*Beat.*) Where the fuck have you been?

ARJUN: (*Excited.*) Something's happened, Bronagh. We were on our way to Chippy. We saw lights in the field. Sadie was begging me to let her go and I thought…I just thought why not? I mean…it could have been nothing, but what if… I was with her after all… We went into the field and what it was… a small crowd – shining torches, singing songs and Sadie was fine. She was fine and then…

BRONAGH: What?

ARJUN: She started gazing at the hollow of this tree.

The offstage crowd start singing Ave Maria – the song of Lourdes version.

MEERA: I know the one.

ARJUN: And you could tell…from her eyes…there was definitely something.

BRONAGH: Where is she?

ARJUN: She's here Bronagh with friends.

BRONAGH makes to go into the field.

Wait!

BRONAGH: I want to see my daughter

ARJUN: Not like this.

BRONAGH: Move!

ARJUN: Bronagh –

BRONAGH: Move, I said! (*She pushes violently past him and walks off stage.*)

MEERA: Wait, son!

ARJUN: What's she going to do?

MEERA: What are you going to do?

ARJUN: Something.

MEERA: Stay calm.

ARJUN: But, what about Sadie –

MEERA: She'll handle it.

ARJUN: There was something in that field.

MEERA: I believe you.

ARJUN: I couldn't see it, but the atmosphere was electric.

MEERA: And Sadie's ok?

ARJUN: She's fine. She's chatting and laughing.

Raised voices offstage. BRONAGH shouting.

BRONAGH: (*Offstage.*) WHERE IS SHE?! WHERE THE FUCK IS SHE?

The offstage crowd stop singing.

ARJUN: It's kicking off.

ARJUN goes off after BRONAGH. We hear him offstage calming her down.

BARRY: Do you not want to go yourself?

MEERA: And make it worse? Oh! This is mad!

BARRY: The girl having visions?

MEERA: No – us, Barry. So long it's been since someone even made a pass at me (*Beat.*) 1956. Shivaji Park swimming pool, Bombay and that was only once before I was married.

BARRY: To him?

MEERA: Hut! He was the swimming pool attendant.

BARRY: But, you still remember it?

MEERA: How can I forget? He crashed his teeth on mine.

He laughs.

It's not funny.

BARRY: It is.

MEERA: Ok it is.

BARRY: It's been a while for me too. Not quite 1956, but –

MEERA: Why Barry?

BARRY: I don't know. There have been women, but they've never stayed. Either that or I've run away. Perhaps I'm tangled in the head – I don't know. What I do know is that today was one of the best days I've ever had. And I'm sorry –

MEERA: For what?

BARRY: I just wanted you Meera…and, the truth is it's…it's been a while.

MEERA: Aha.

BARRY: Quite a while so… I was a bit…excited…

MEERA: Aha.

BARRY: If we did it again, I'm sure…you know –

MEERA: What?

BARRY: I'd…you know…go on longer I mean…what is it they say practice make perfect…no, I didn't mean that.

MEERA: It was perfect.

BARRY: Was it?

MEERA: Yes.

BARRY: Cos I think you're gorgeous, Meera.

MEERA: Do you?

BARRY: I think you're the most gorgeous woman in the world.

MEERA: I'm not.

BARRY: All the time at the lake, I couldn't stop thinking about you, your beautiful face, your eyes. I wanted to touch you.

MEERA: Now you're embarrassing me.

BARRY: Sorry…

MEERA: Continue.

BARRY: I don't know what to say now.

MEERA: You were doing well.

BARRY: I'm just a simple man from the country –

MEERA: Aha.

BARRY: I like simple people.

MEERA: What?

BARRY: I mean your eyes are like…brown.

MEERA: Yeah?

BARRY: They're brown.

MEERA: Aha?

BARRY: They're dark brown.

MEERA: You're just repeating yourself now.

BARRY: I've lost it.

MEERA: Say anything. The first thing in your mind.

BARRY: I can't. I have butterflies in my stomach.

MEERA: So, do I.

BARRY: Mine are really swarming now.

They kiss passionately. ARJUN and BRONAGH return from offstage.

ARJUN: (*Offstage.*) Relax!

BRONAGH: (*Offstage.*) Where the fuck is she Arjun?

BARRY and MEERA break off.

ARJUN: She was just there.

BRONAGH: She's not there now.

ARJUN: She probably got talking to someone.

BRONAGH: Barry, I need to use your phone.

BARRY: Surely.

ARJUN: What are you going to do?

BRONAGH: I'm calling the guard.

ARJUN: They'll laugh at you, Bronagh.

BRONAGH: Let them laugh.

ARJUN: Maybe she's gone into the shrine.

BRONAGH: How could you do this?

ARJUN: I did what I thought was best.

BRONAGH: For who?

ARJUN: For her.

BRONAGH: And for you.

ARJUN: What?

Beat.

BRONAGH: I read your story Arjun. I read it off the computer. All about a family on holiday in a caravan and a little girl who sees an angel in a field, and granny who's sick and a poor put upon writer, but the character that most intrigued me was the wife. What a creation Arjun! What a bitch!

ARJUN: It's not you.

BRONAGH: You even call her Bronwyn.

ARJUN: It's what writers do. We take real life and reforge it in the furnace of imagination.

BRONAGH: Fuck you! You told me you were writing about the Asian diaspora.

ARJUN: I didn't mean to…it just flowed.

BRONAGH: And then you take her into the field?

ARJUN: Bronagh –

BRONAGH: Stopped flowing had it?

ARJUN: No.

BRONAGH: Move!

ARJUN: Not until you hear me out –

BRONAGH: Move I said!

She pushes past him and into the office.

MEERA: So, you're writing about us?

ARJUN: No, it's loosely based on events –

BARRY: Am I in it?

ARJUN: No and it wouldn't be you anyway, it would be a character –

BARRY: So, are they in a caravan park?

ARJUN: Yes.

BARRY: Is there not someone who runs it?

ARJUN: Yes.

BARRY: What his name?

ARJUN: Does it matter?

BARRY: Is it Barry?

ARJUN: Barney – it's only a working name.

BARRY: You should call him Laurence –

ARJUN: What?

BARRY: I always liked the name Laurence.

ARJUN: It's not you, Barney.

BARRY: Barry.

ARJUN: That's what I meant.

MEERA: So, is it a drama you're writing about us?

ARJUN: It's not about us.

MEERA: I don't mind if it is Arjun.

ARJUN: It isn't.

MEERA: But is it a drama I'm asking you?

ARJUN: It's a short story.

MEERA: Make it a drama.

ARJUN: Can we change the subject please?

MEERA: Dramas are better.

ARJUN: Now she's giving me literary advice.

MEERA: And dramas can be shown on TV.

ARJUN: Now it's going to be on TV.

MEERA: Why not? Send to Ashok Prashar – he works at Zee TV.

ARJUN: It's not going to be on Zee TV.

MEERA: Why not?

ARJUN: It's got no songs in it for a start.

MEERA: Not all dramas on Zee have songs. (*Beat.*) Mind you if it had songs –

ARJUN: Forget it!

BARRY: Can Barney have a song?

ARJUN: No.

BARRY: Why not?

ARJUN: He's got throat cancer.

MEERA: That's a horrible thing to say and Barry's got such a lovely voice. Sing that one you were singing at the lake.

BARRY: Ah no!

MEERA: Don't be shy, Barry.

ARJUN: Look it's not a drama and there are no songs.

MEERA: We're just giving you ideas Arjun.

ARJUN: I don't want them.

MEERA: It's the simple ideas that make the big bucks. Look at *Bend It Like Beckham.*

BARRY: (*Sings.*) Her eyes they shone like the diamond
　　You'd think she was queen of the land
　　And her hair hung over her shoulder
　　Tied up in a black velvet band.

　　BRONAGH comes out of the office.

BRONAGH: What's this? Song for Europe?

MEERA: What did they say?

BRONAGH: Nothing. Sit tight.

MEERA: They're right.

BRONAGH: It's easy for you. It's not your daughter who's missing.

MEERA: Look, I am a mother too, Bronagh.

BRONAGH: When she gets back, we're off.

MEERA: It's ok. You have a lovely daughter. You're blessed. So is
　　she.

BRONAGH: She is not blessed.

MEERA: Then what happened in that field?

BRONAGH: The God squad got hysterical.

MEERA: No, before that, when I was in the field with her.

BRONAGH: Oh that!

MEERA: I felt the power she had.

BRONAGH: You felt what you wanted to feel.

MEERA: I couldn't walk. I couldn't breathe.

BRONAGH: You thought you couldn't.

MEERA: Twice I was rushed to hospital last year.

BRONAGH: I know. I was there in the middle of the night when
　　he got the phone calls, when he dropped everything to be
　　by your side. I told him, 'Go! Be with her,' and both times
　　he came back saying you were sitting up in bed, asking if
　　they'd given him food on the plane. You didn't sound like
　　a dying woman to me. Not like my own Mam at the end,
　　when she couldn't even hold my hand. I said I would dance
　　on her grave, but when I saw her… I knew. We all knew.
　　And the nurses just bustling around like normal. See, it's not

some Bollywood movie with a hundred false endings. It's simple. Final. No comebacks. But, with you there are always comebacks.

MEERA: What do you mean?

BRONAGH: You weren't dying. You were never dying.

MEERA: Seriously ill I was.

BRONAGH: You were lonely.

MEERA: The doctors said –

BRONAGH: You'll outlive us all Meera, though you'll talk about death till your dying day –

ARJUN: So, she was lying – pretending all this time?

BRONAGH: The way a person feels means everything.

ARJUN: She's a different person Bronagh.

BRONAGH: That's not a miracle.

ARJUN: To me it is.

BRONAGH: And it's not Sadie's doing – that much I know.

ARJUN: All I know is they went into that field –

BRONAGH: Just because they went into that field, then she got better, doesn't mean Sadie made her better.

ARJUN: Who made her better then?

BRONAGH: You really don't know, do you?

ARJUN: What?

BRONAGH: (*Pointing to BARRY.*) Ask him.

ARJUN: What? Barry?

BRONAGH: Yes.

ARJUN: What are you talking about?

BRONAGH: Ask him what they were doing earlier. Ask him!

ARJUN: (*To BARRY.*) What's she on about?

BARRY: Nothing.

BRONAGH: Nothing was it?

BARRY: It was between us. Between your Mam and I.

BRONAGH: You can say that again.

ARJUN: Am I missing something?

MEERA: We were having sex ok?

ARJUN: Sorry?

MEERA: We were having sex.

ARJUN: You were having sex with Barry?

MEERA: Yes.

ARJUN: You were having sex with Barry?

MEERA: We've become close.

ARJUN: You were having sex with Barry?

MEERA: Yes.

   Beat.

ARJUN: You were having sex with – ?

MEERA: What are you – a broken record?

ARJUN: I'm trying to get my head around it.

MEERA: I'm a woman. He's a man.

ARJUN: But...why?

MEERA: I wanted to.

ARJUN: But...he's the janitor.

MEERA: Who cares? (*Beat.*) Anyway he's the manager of the caravan park.

ARJUN: Some manager!

MEERA: What's the big deal anyway?

ARJUN: Do you think it's appropriate at your age?

MEERA: Oh get lost!

ARJUN: Are you in love?

MEERA: Who are you – my father?

ARJUN: It's my father I'm thinking about. He'd be turning in his grave.

MEERA: Let him spin.

ARJUN: This is weird.

MEERA: Get used to it.

ARJUN: You're not going to do it again?

MEERA: It's only sex. You have sex, don't you?

ARJUN: I'm not having this conversation.

MEERA: But it's ok isn't it?

ARJUN: No! It's fucking weird.

BRONAGH: There you go. That's what's put the spring back in her step.

MEERA: Very good Bronagh. You know everything, don't you?

BRONAGH: I don't know where my daughter is.

MEERA: But there's more here than even you know.

The next speeches till SADIE's entrance can run into/over each other.

BRONAGH: (*To ARJUN.*) I can't believe you brought her into that field.

MEERA: And there's more in that field.

BRONAGH: ...when you knew what I said –

ARJUN: She's ok.

MEERA: Why are people following her?

BRONAGH: (*To ARJUN.*) She's missing, you arsehole.

MEERA: People aren't stupid. They don't just follow anyone.

ARJUN: Why are you panicking?

BRONAGH: (*To ARJUN.*) I could fucking kill you.

MEERA: They believe in her. They need to believe.

BRONAGH: If anything's happened to her –

MEERA: They need hope.

ARJUN: Nothing has happened to her.

MEERA: And that girl, your girl is creating hope in that field.

BRONAGH: Oh fuck off!

ARJUN: Bronagh!

BRONAGH: (*To MEERA.*) You're half the fucking problem here.

MEERA: Mind you language.

BRONAGH: Or what'll you do? Slipper me?

MEERA: Don't tempt me.

BRONAGH: He may be afraid of your slippers. I'm not.

MEERA: You should be. I'll knock your teeth out with them.

BRONAGH: I'll make you eat the fucking slippers first.

MEERA: The first bite will be your hand only – right to the bone.

BRONAGH: How you gonna do that if I use a brick to straighten out your teeth?

MEERA: I'll brick you bitch! I'll brick you through the fucking brain!

BRONAGH: Not if I drive the fucking caravan over your fucking head you won't!

BARRY: Will you pack it in? Nobody's driving anything over anybody's –

BRONAGH: Well, I'm glad to see the old Meera's back.

MEERA: She brings it out in me.

BRONAGH: The real Meera.

By now SADIE has come on.

SADIE: Jesus! The gobs on you lot'll wake the dead.

BRONAGH: Sweetheart! Where have you been?

SADIE: I was only in the next caravan with Heather having a biscuit (*Showing them a figurine.*) Look what she gave me – a black saint. We don't know his name. I'm calling him Saint Arjun.

BRONAGH: We're leaving.

SADIE: What? Now?

BRONAGH: Yes.

SADIE: I can't Mam.

BRONAGH: Sadie –

SADIE: I have to go into the field.

Beat.

BRONAGH: No.

SADIE: She's waiting for me in the field.

BRONAGH: Forget the field, Sadie!

SADIE: How can I Mam? She's my friend, my angel.

BRONAGH: No.

SADIE: How else did I survive when everyone else died? I was in that car. But, she was there with me.

BRONAGH: No.

SADIE: She pulled me out.

BRONAGH: Get in the caravan Sadie. We're going.

SADIE: To Galway?

BRONAGH: Yes.

SADIE: I know why you're taking me to there Mam. I know about the shrink.

BRONAGH: Who told you? (*To ARJUN.*) Did you tell her?

SADIE: I know things Mam.

BRONAGH: I just want you talk to him.

SADIE: What's he going to say that any of the others haven't said?

BRONAGH: Just talk to him.

MEERA: Why don't you talk to him?

BRONAGH: Shut up!

MEERA: You need it more than her.

BRONAGH: (*To MEERA.*) SHUT THE FUCK UP!

SADIE moves towards the field.

SADIE: I have to go now Mam.

BRONAGH: You are not going into that field.

SADIE: I have to Mum.

BRONAGH: Get into the caravan.

SADIE: No.

BRONAGH: Get into the caravan.

SADIE: No.

BRONAGH: GET INTO THE FUCKING CARAVAN I SAID!

She slaps SADIE hard across the face. SADIE holds her face.

ARJUN: Bronagh!

BARRY: Christ!

MEERA: Arre! Hey Baghwan!

SADIE: You hit me Mam.

BRONAGH: I'm sorry darling. I'm sorry…

MEERA: (*Embracing SADIE.*) Poor girl!

BRONAGH: I'm trying to protect you, Sadie.

MEERA: She's fine.

BRONAGH: She is not fine.

MEERA: She's perfect, Bronagh.

BRONAGH: Then why is she talking to a dead girl?

MEERA: What?

BRONAGH: Why is she leaving messages for her?

MEERA: What?

BRONAGH: Tell them Sadie or will I?

Beat.

Derbhle Kelly was in that car. You and Derbhle, and Noel
– on a little jaunt in Noel's brother's car. Noel showing off,
putting his foot down, but he clipped the curb, the car flipped,
must have ruptured the fuel tank – the whole thing in flames.
They died – Derbhle and Noel. They burned. But, you were
thrown clear. How? Why? I don't know. Found outside.
Hardly had a bruise on you, but these things happen. Bomb
blasts in Iraq which rip twenty people apart, but leave one
person standing, untouched. Random, unbelievable acts, but
possible, totally explicable… And when I got you home, you
wouldn't talk. You wouldn't cry. Not a word you said for days,
until I brought you the note.

ARJUN: What note?

BRONAGH: The note, she'd forgotten about, left on the kitchen
counter.

SADIE: Shut up!

BRONAGH: (*To ARJUN.*) Remember that argument we'd had about her mobile bill – 150 Euro's on calls to Derbhle. A real shouting match and she said she'd make me sorry. Well, this was it…

ARJUN: What?

BRONAGH: …she was going away. Never coming back.

SADIE: You promised.

BRONAGH: And when I brought you the note, you did cry and I held you in my arms and you talked to me and it was about the last time that we did talk, really talk. You told me you made Derbhle get in that car. She didn't even want to.

SADIE: Shut up! Shut up!

BRONAGH: And that's why you're calling her up now. And that's who it is in that field. Not the Virgin Mary or anyone else, but a new best friend to replace the one you think you killed.

SADIE: Shut up I said!

BRONAGH: But you didn't kill her, Sadie. It doesn't matter that you said you wouldn't be her friend if she didn't get in that car.

SADIE: You promised!

BRONAGH: It doesn't matter you were angry with the pair of them.

SADIE: You promised!

BRONAGH: It was not your fault, Sadie.

SADIE: How do you know?

BRONAGH: It was their choice –

SADIE: But, I knew what was going to happen that day.

BRONAGH: No, Sadie.

SADIE: I knew. I did. Because I know things.

BRONAGH: No, Sadie –

SADIE: But, I was so angry with them that I wanted it to happen.

BRONAGH: No –

SADIE: I just didn't know that I would survive. And I wish I hadn't. I wish I hadn't.

She runs into the caravan.

BRONAGH: (*Trying to hold her.*) Sadie!

SADIE goes into the caravan, closes the door.

Please sweetheart. We have to talk.

BRONAGH put her head against the closed door.

I'm coming in Sadie. I'm coming in to talk to you.

ARJUN: Why didn't you tell me this?

BRONAGH: So you could make notes? Put it in your story?

ARJUN: No.

BRONAGH: You don't care.

ARJUN: I do.

BRONAGH: You're a fucking liar.

ARJUN: Bronagh!

BRONAGH: Stay away from us.

ARJUN: I want to make it better. How can I –

BRONAGH: Delete that story.

ARJUN: I'll do that.

BRONAGH: And burn those notebooks.

ARJUN: My books?

BRONAGH: If we mean anything to you –

ARJUN: Bronagh, I can't destroy my books.

BRONAGH: Then stay away from us.

ARJUN: Bronagh –

She goes into the caravan.

BARRY: She'll feel different in the morning.

ARJUN: She won't be here in the morning.

BARRY: Give her space.

ARJUN: That's it. I've lost her.

BARRY: No –

ARJUN: I've lost her. I've lost her.

MEERA: Well, plenty more fish in the –

ARJUN: Shut up!!

> *Beat.*

> I'll get a hotel for the night.

BARRY: Call the Belgrove. Use the phone in the office if you like.

MEERA: And just one room son, for yourself.

ARJUN: Where are you going to…? (*He answers his own question and exits.*)

MEERA: God! What a mess! I should have been here with them.

BARRY: Instead of at the lake with me?

MEERA: But, I'm old Barry.

BARRY: I don't care what age you are.

MEERA: I came here to die. I dreamed about it.

BARRY: And perhaps you did die.

MEERA: What?

BARRY: The old you. Perhaps that's what your dream meant. All my life I've been waiting. I've spent years sitting in that office, waiting, I'd given up, lost hope, but there must have been some little part of me, some tiny grain that still believed, that needed to believe…in you. Do you not feel it Meera?

MEERA: Yes. (*Beat.*) Do these things happen Barry?

BARRY: I believe they do.

> *Lights fade.*

SCENE 4

The next morning SADIE is at the table outside the caravan on her mobile phone. Her manner is playful, yet on the edge. It could be more like a direct address to us.

SADIE: (*On mobile.*) So, there was this woman called Sati and this God called Shiva. Well, not exactly cos she was actually the Goddess Shakti reborn in human form – but let's not go there yet. Anyway Shiva and Sati fell in love and got married. But, her father – let's call him Ken – was not happy cos Shiva was a bit odd. In fact mostly he sat on a mountaintop, wearing only skulls and snake skins, and all he did was think about the essential nature of the Universe…so, I'm kinda guessing he wasn't big on pleasantries, which got up Ken's nose. And, one time Ken had this party and he didn't invite Shiva or Sati. And in the middle of the party was this massive open fire. But, Sati turned up anyway, and when she saw Ken, she goes, 'Da, why didn't you invite me and Shiva to the party?' and Ken goes, 'Cos he's a scruff and eejit,' and everyone had a good laugh at Shiva's expense and Sati stepped into the fire…she stepped into the fire and burned herself alive. And Shiva hearing this, came storming in and wrecked the place and cut off Ken's head, which definitely put a damper on things. But, just then Shiva steps into the fire and lifting Sati's dead body, he starts to dance. (*SADIE starts to move slowly, rhythmically, maybe to a low rhythmic tabla.*) And the dance he does is the Dance of Destruction, which brings about the end of the universe. And he dances faster and faster (*She dances faster and more frenetically.*) till this other God – Vishnu – throws his golden disc, which is razor sharp, and cuts Sati's body into pieces and each piece falls in a different part of India and in each place a shrine is built where they worship the Goddess Shakti – remember her at the beginning? – and so Shiva stops dancing. But I'm not. (*She continues to dance and spin faster and faster, the music louder.*) See that was it. Remember yer man outside Eason's. That's what he's doing, Derbhle, he's doing Shiva's dance. I know it. I'm sure of it, either that or he's just completely fucking mad. Another Dublin loony talking to himself and pissing in his trousers. And he'll end up in a mental home I bet, locked up in a white room in a white building. That's where he'll end up. That's where they all end up in the end. (*She falls. Beat.*) Recently, I've been thinking about Scandinavia. I've always wanted to go. I imagine it's big and white. Is it like that where you are? Is it big and white? Is it simple? Why don't you call me and tell me what it's like? Why don't you ever call me? Is it cos you're mad at me? Is that it? I've said sorry. What else can I do? It was always you and me, Derbhle, you and me, and then suddenly it was you and Noel and I knew you and me were finished and I didn't want that cos I only had you. Who else likes me? Who ever has? I'm so alone. Alone with questions in my head going round and round, driving me mad. Is it you in that field? It doesn't look like you, but then maybe it is, maybe you've come back. Maybe… Maybe… If it is, just say. Please say. Or call me. Why don't you call me? Call me. Please… Call me.

BRONAGH: (*From inside.*) Sadie.

SADIE hides the mobile. BRONAGH comes out of the caravan.

Have you brushed your teeth?

SADIE does not respond.

Cos we have to go.

SADIE does not respond.

We've a bit of a drive to Galway.

SADIE does not respond.

You're going to have to talk to me sometime Sadie. We've five years together at least.

SADIE does not respond.

I've said sorry about what I did. How many times –

SADIE goes into the toilets. ARJUN comes out of the caravan. He is carrying a big black holdall full of stuff.

ARJUN: You ok?

BRONAGH: Grand. My marriage is breaking up, my daughter hates me –

ARJUN: She doesn't hate you.

BRONAGH: What happened here? We were happy enough. An ordinary happiness we had, the kind which drives you up the wall, but that was ok –

By now ARJUN is at the table and making notes in his book.

BRONAGH: You're not taking notes on this, are you?

ARJUN: I've had an idea.

BRONAGH: This is my life, Arjun. It's not a story.

ARJUN: It's something new.

BRONAGH: What?

Beat.

ARJUN: It's about a man who's in the middle of everything: his family, his work, heaven, hell, God, nothing being pulled about by the current of competing ideas.

BRONAGH: Right.

ARJUN: I'm calling it 'Middleman' – working title. Because the point is when it begins he's in the middle, but it's an odyssey – a quest to get out of the middle, to find some answers. You think it's shit.

BRONAGH: No, but –

ARJUN: …What?

BRONAGH: Is it that important to you?

ARJUN: What?

BRONAGH: This writing?

ARJUN: It's this middle, Bronagh. It's killing me.

SADIE comes out of the toilet. She sees them.

SADIE: (*To ARJUN.*) You off then?

ARJUN: Yes.

SADIE: Bye. (*Beat.*) I suppose I will miss you.

ARJUN: Yeah?

SADIE: Sure, who will I wind up now?

ARJUN: You'll find someone.

SADIE: Not like you.

ARJUN: You may even find that special someone you enjoy winding up more than me.

SADIE: And we'll have kids – five girls – and we'll all wind him up.

ARJUN: And he'll lock himself in a wooden box.

SADIE: And we'll position it in front of the TV.

ARJUN: And feed him through a slot.

SADIE: And we'll all live happily ever after.

> *They laugh. Suddenly SADIE hugs ARJUN tightly.*

> Don't go!

ARJUN: I have to.

SADIE: Don't walk out on us.

ARJUN: I'm not –

SADIE: Please, Da.

ARJUN: Da?

SADIE: I mean… (*Beat.*)

ARJUN: I'll be around, Sadie.

SADIE: That's nothing, Arjun. That's nothing.

> *SADIE heads off towards the field.*

BRONAGH: Where are you going?

> *SADIE doesn't respond.*

> I'm speaking to you Sadie.

SADIE: I need some air.

BRONAGH: You are not going into that field.

SADIE: Stop me.

BRONAGH: I know you were talking on that mobile again.

SADIE: So?

BRONAGH: You can't do that anymore.

SADIE: Yes, I can.

BRONAGH: No, Sadie. You can't even pretend cos I had it disconnected this morning.

SADIE: What?

BRONAGH: You heard me.

> *SADIE takes it out and looks at it. She tries it and is shocked.*

> I'm trying to help you, Sadie.

SADIE: (*Tossing it on the floor.*) Fucking keep the mobile. I'll still talk to Derbhle. I'll find a way.

BRONAGH: I'm on your side, don't you understand?

SADIE: Yeah, right.

BRONAGH: I'd do anything for you. I'd die for you.

SADIE: Then prove it.

BRONAGH: What?

SADIE: Cos that's the best thing you could do for me, right now. And see if you did, I wouldn't be sad. I'd dance on your grave.

BRONAGH: You don't mean that.

SADIE: I'd piss on it.

BRONAGH: Come here! Come back here!

SADIE: Or what you going to do? Hit me?

SADIE goes off. BRONAGH sits at the table.

BRONAGH: What should I do?

ARJUN: Nothing.

BRONAGH: Nothing? Do nothing? That's your job. Sitting there being nice. I'm the one who keeps her on the straight and narrow, who frets herself half to death, who cares.

ARJUN: I care Bronagh.

BRONAGH: No it's all about you – your greater meaning, your higher purpose, except it's not is it? It's not meaning you're after.

ARJUN: What is it then?

BRONAGH: I don't know Arjun. Maybe you want to be a great man. Have people read your books. When you're dead, maybe you want a statue put up in your honour. But, the chances are you'll just become one of the millions who spend their lives in front rooms, in libraries making work nobody reads, and even if I'm wrong, even if something does sell, you'll still be searching Arjun, because that stuff means nothing. We create meaning. We put it into things. I can hardly think of a thing which has meaning in itself – except perhaps family, except the ones you love –

ARJUN: (*Referring to SADIE.*) Then why are you pushing her away?

BRONAGH: I'm not pushing her away.

ARJUN: You can't even see it.

BRONAGH: Oh fuck off! Fuck off! Just fuck off!

ARJUN takes his bag and is on his way.

Are you're just going to fuck off?

ARJUN: It's what you want.

BRONAGH: I just want my daughter back.

BRONAGH goes into the caravan. ARJUN sits down. BARRY comes on.

BARRY: Is it safe to come through?

ARJUN is silent.

Your Mam's here. We're going to Knocknacree.

ARJUN: Right.

BARRY: Just popped in to say hello, goodbye, have a last look at that toilet.

ARJUN: Don't let me stand in your way.

MEERA comes on.

MEERA: Son? You look shattered.

ARJUN: I didn't sleep.

MEERA: We neither. Not a wink.

ARJUN: Why? Actually, no! Forget it…don't answer that question.

MEERA: No, we were talking into the night.

ARJUN: Right.

MEERA: But we're feeling ok for it, aren't we Barry?

BARRY: We're feeling grand.

ARJUN: Good.

BARRY: I'll er…go and check on that toilet.

BARRY goes.

ARJUN: So you're going on a little trip, I hear?

MEERA: Knocknacree. Just today, tonight.

ARJUN: What about your things?

MEERA: All I need are the clothes on my back. And yaw'l? Leaving today?

ARJUN: They are.

MEERA: You're not going with them?

ARJUN: No.

MEERA: You and she still fighting?

ARJUN: Yes.

MEERA: You want me to talk to her for you?

ARJUN: No.

MEERA: You can come with us to Knocknacree –

ARJUN: I think I'll pass.

MEERA: So, what are you going to do?

ARJUN: Hang around the souvenir shops.

MEERA: Arjun –

ARJUN: I'll be fine.

MEERA: Will you?

ARJUN: Yes, will you?

MEERA: Oh yes, Barry's going to show me Ireland.

ARJUN: Be careful, won't you?

MEERA: What do you mean?

ARJUN: Be safe.

MEERA: You mean condoms?

ARJUN: No, I do not mean bloody condoms.

MEERA: They've got quite expensive, haven't they?

ARJUN: I'm not having this conversation.

MEERA: Relax.

ARJUN: I mean in general – you'll look after yourself.

MEERA: Yes.

ARJUN: That's ok then. That's all I want to know.

MEERA: Ok.

ARJUN: If you need me, if you need anything –

MEERA: It's a small world Arjun – mobile phones.

ARJUN: And if he asks you to marry him –

MEERA laughs.

What?

MEERA: We're having fun Arjun – that's all.

ARJUN: Fine. Have a good time.

MEERA: You're still my boy. You'll always be my boy.

She puts a hand on his arm. They embrace. BARRY comes out.

BARRY: Oh!

MEERA: No, it's ok.

BARRY: No, I'm jealous.

MEERA: What?

BARRY: Another man holding you.

MEERA: You can hold me any time.

BARRY: Well, the toilet's working like a dream.

ARJUN: Yeah?

BARRY: God knows how. I just used the plunger like before.

MEERA: Perhaps you're plunging it differently. (*Suggestive.*) You're very good at plunging.

ARJUN: Right. I'm off!

MEERA: I'm only pulling your leg, Arjun.

ARJUN: No, there's something I have to do. Take care of her Barry.

BARRY: I will.

MEERA: I'll call you.

ARJUN heads off into the field.

So, is it a long drive to Knocknacree?

BARRY: A good few hours. The B and B looks nice.

MEERA: And Drumcliff tomorrow?

BARRY: Aye, where Yeats is buried.

MEERA: Cast a cold eye
  On Life, On death
  Horseman pass by.

BARRY: You're amazing Meera. You know Yeats as well.

MEERA: I read it in the guidebook, Barry.

BARRY: Oh forget that! I'm going to show you the real Ireland.
  The place I know.

MEERA: I can't wait.

BARRY: Then you can show me India.

MEERA: That's not fair. It's bigger.

BARRY: Sure, we have all time in the world.

MEERA: Do we? Really?

BARRY: We have the time we have and that's enough.

  They kiss.

  Plus the fact each minute with you seems like an hour.

  Beat.

MEERA: That's not a nice thing to say.

BARRY: No, I didn't mean that.

MEERA: You should work on your lines.

  BRONAGH comes out of the caravan.

BARRY: I'll go start the car.

  BARRY goes.

MEERA: Arjun tells me you're still fighting.

BRONAGH: It's over.

MEERA: I'm sorry.

BRONAGH: Are you? Isn't this is what you wanted?

MEERA: No.

BRONAGH: It's not been a bad trip for you. You got a man, got rid
  of me.

MEERA: You can't make it up – the two of you?

BRONAGH: He's more interested in writing.

MEERA: Oh come on that's a small thing. You can't break up over a small thing.

BRONAGH: We're supposed to be buying a house.

MEERA: Do you love him?

BRONAGH: I don't want to talk about this.

MEERA: Don't be proud, Bronagh. You'll regret it.

BRONAGH: Why are you here?

MEERA: To say goodbye.

BRONAGH: Goodbye.

MEERA: To Sadie also.

BRONAGH: She's in the field.

MEERA: You must learn to talk to her, Bronagh.

BRONAGH: Look, I don't need your advice.

MEERA: Or you'll lose her.

BARRY beeps offstage.

BRONAGH: There's your lift.

MEERA: Listen to her. Listen to what she says and tell her you love her.

BRONAGH: You think I haven't done that?

MEERA: Keep saying it until she hears you. And maybe…

BRONAGH: What?!

MEERA: Maybe…imagine there's something in what she's telling you.

BRONAGH: What? Visions? Ghosts?

MEERA: I know a bit of you wants to believe her. Even just a tiny grain.

BRONAGH: Goodbye Meera.

MEERA: It's there Bronagh – that grain. I know it.

BRONAGH: Goodbye.

MEERA goes.

And good luck. (*She sits on the step, at the end of her tether now.*) Perhaps she's right. Perhaps I should believe in you. I never could before, but perhaps you are... And see – if you are... this I know: you're not good, you're not kind. You're a big cruel bastard! Cos only a bastard could do the things you do, or watch them play out and never stir. Is it a laugh you're having? Watching it all fall apart? Is it like You've Been Framed except with people's lives? I'm losing everything here and you're laughing. (*Rage.*) Well, laugh! Laugh ya bastard! Laugh!

ARJUN walks back on followed by SADIE.

(*Drying her tears fast.*) What's this? A deposition?

ARJUN: She wants to say something.

Beat.

SADIE: I'm sorry that I said I'd piss on your grave. I won't. I won't even dance on it.

ARJUN: And?

SADIE: That's all I'm saying.

BRONAGH: (*Going to embrace her.*) Oh sweetheart!

SADIE: Don't touch me. I didn't say it's all ok, but I won't piss on your grave.

BRONAGH: Ok.

SADIE goes into the caravan.

What did you say to her?

ARJUN: I just talked to her Bronagh. She wants to believe in you.

BRONAGH: Does she?

ARJUN: You two have some serious talking to do.

BRONAGH: Yeah.

ARJUN: Best get started.

BRONAGH: Two heads are better than one, Arjun.

ARJUN: What?

BRONAGH: Help me.

ARJUN: I can't.

BRONAGH: The writing thing…if you really have to do it… I mean your 'Middleman' idea, perhaps there's something in it. We're all in the middle aren't we? I am with her. Cos she's saying these things that go against everything I believe, but I want to believe in her and I don't want to lose her.

ARJUN: Go in and tell her that.

BRONAGH: Come with me.

ARJUN: No.

BRONAGH: She listens to you Arjun.

ARJUN: She listened to me this time, but that was fluke.

BRONAGH: Please Arjun.

ARJUN: This is between you and her now.

BRONAGH: And what about you? Off to win a Pulitzer, are you?

ARJUN: I'm not a writer, Bronagh. I'm not going to win any prizes.

BRONAGH: …So?

ARJUN: But the doubts are real and they're not just about work. They're about everything now. They're about us.

BRONAGH: What?

ARJUN: There's something wrong here, Bronagh. I think it could be us.

BRONAGH: No.

ARJUN: Yes.

BRONAGH: Is that what you think? What you really think?

ARJUN: Yes.

BRONAGH: Then, you'd better go.

ARJUN: Bronagh –

BRONAGH: Just go.

ARJUN picks up his bag. He's starts to leave.

But, it's here, Arjun. We're here. We're all the meaning you need.

ARJUN goes. BRONAGH pulls herself together now, aware she has an uphill struggle. She turns to go into the caravan. Suddenly the phone rings. At first she can't believe it. She thought it was disconnected. She picks up the phone. A light shines from the direction of the shrine. The sun coming out from behind clouds? She studies the phone, letting it ring for a long time before putting it to her ear.

(*With trepidation.*) Hello?

Blackout.